Targum Jonathan
to the Prophets

Pinkhos Churgin

Alpha Editions

This edition published in 2019

ISBN : 9789353955519

Design and Setting By
Alpha Editions
email - alphaedis@gmail.com

YALE ORIENTAL SERIES — RESEARCHES XIV

TARGUM JONATHAN
TO THE PROPHETS

BY
PINKHOS CHURGIN

NEW HAVEN
YALE UNIVERSITY PRESS
MDCCCCVII

Fa

GT

CONTENTS

7

THE HISTORICAL BACKGROUND OF
TARGUM JONATHAN

The Aramaic rendering of the Prophets belongs to the earliest translations of the Bible which have come down to us. Its importance for the textual investigation and early Biblical interpretation cannot be overestimated. While the targumist makes little display of critical study in rendering intricate passages, and while he does not pretend to present a minutely literal translation of the Hebrew text, his reverence for the letter and transmitted reading of the text must be far have exceeded that of the Greek and Syriac translators. At the same time his translation is doubtlessly based on a sounder and exacter understanding of both the etymology and usages of the Hebrew language. Again, its value may be said to rest in the fact that, forming a distinct and independent rendering of the text, it presents a helpful source in establishing the principles pursued in the early translations. A good many emendations and assumed violations of the Hebrew text on the sole basis of the translations, so eagerly sought by the modern Biblical scholar, would thus be completely done away with. It is also a mine of Agadic exegesis, to which, in most instances, parallels are preserved in the extant sources. It cannot fail to be of considerable importance for the history of that vast literature, giving in this connection new and vivid emphasis to the religious, national and political state of mind of that age in Palestine.

The authorship of the Targum to the Prophets has been the object of protracted and diverse discussion. Tradition ascribes it to Jonathan b. Uziel, the most prominent disciple of Hillel, of the first century. This single mention in the Talmud of the authorship of Jonathan and the mystic manner in which it is related, can hardly help solve the problem. There is, furthermore, the astounding fact that in the parallel passage in the

Yerushalmi [1] there is complete silence of this tradition of the Babli.[2] Had this tradition been common, there could have been no possible reason for the Yerushalmi to ignore the work of the distinguished and holy Jonathan, who "when he discussed the law, a bird flying near him would be burned".[3]

The Talmudic tradition mentions Aquila's translation. Both Talmudim have set monuments to the Seventy. Is it because the Targum was originated on Palestinian soil, extensively used and known in Palestine, forming even a necessary part in the worship, that they failed to be impressed by it?

So the inference was drawn that the Aramaic version of the Bible fell in disfavor with the authorities in Palestine who, how-ever, were distinctly pleased with the Greek translation, particu-larly the Greek version of Aquila.[4] The alleged reasons for

---

1) Y. Megilla 1, 9.

2) Babli Meg. 3b. Blau's contention (J. Q. R., v. 9, p. 738) has no foundation. Cases of disagreement in assigning the author of a say-ing are numerous. It needs no explanation and consequently cannot be made a basis for a new theory.

3) Suk. 28a; Baba Bathra 134a; Y. Nedarim 5, 6.

4) Berliner (Onkelos 108-110) has even the idea of a complete suppression of the official Targumim in Palestine. Weiss (Dor Dor etc., v. 1, 200) even knows exactly the time when this suppression took place and its author. It was Rabban Gamliel, of whom it is said (Shab. 115a; Tosef. 13 (14) and with some changes in Sof. 5, 15; Y. Shab. 16, 1) that he hid the Targum to Job. So then it was he who put the ban also on the official Targumim. And it was not until the time of R. Akiba that the ban was lifted. This conjecture is read by Weiss into the phrase מי גלה סתרי לבני אדם. It is evident that the whole supposition hinges on the mere finding that Rabban Gamliel forbade the use of a certain particular Targum. That the express mention of the Targum should be taken to indicate that the other Targumim were spared this interdiction seems to have escaped their observation. Furthermore, their theory is exposed to a dangerous contradiction. If the Targum was restored in the time of R. Akiba, what sense could there have been to the contention of R. Chalafta with Gamliel the younger, a contemporary of R. Akiba, with regard to his license with the Targum, and his reminder of R. Gamliel the Elder? They should not have overlooked the remarkable coincidence presented in the story of Gamliel the Elder and his grand-child. In both instances it was the Targum to Job that evoked disfavor.

such a departure will hardly stand their ground. But aside from other considerations, this assertion is flatly contradicted by the very fact that the Aramaic version was not ignored by the Palestinian authorities. Both Onkelos and Jonathan are quoted in the Yerushalmi and Midrashim,[5] while, on the contrary, the genuineness of the quotations from Aquila is doubtful.[6]

It was, then, clearly this Targum which was hit by Rabban Gamliel the Elder, and which was still regarded as forbidden.

There is little to be said of Finn's conjecture (v. 1, 56, דברי הימים) that the suppression of the Targum to the Pent. was due to the intro-duction of the Samaritan Targum with its dangerous divergencies from the Hebrew text. This he attempts to discover in the obscure saying of Mar Zutra (San. 21b).

It needs only to be mentioned that there is not the faintest hint in the Talmud of a suspension of the Targum-reading in the worship, as he would have us believe. Rosenthal (Beth Ha-Midrash 2, 276) takes the view that the reverence in which Aquila's translation was held in Pales-tine was due to the fact that Greek was spoken more than Aramaic in Palestine. It is pure imagination.

5) The reader is referred to Zunz G. V., p. 67, Notes b, c. It should be remarked that the list of citations given by Zunz represents by no means an exhaustive research. It is not my present task to cite the numerous cases which, for some reason or other, he does not cite. Suffice it to state that citations from Onkelos alone in Genesis r. exceed considerably the number of citations from Aquila taken together. Com. Lerner, An. u. Quellen d. Breishit Raba 63-65. His view that the respective citations may not represent actual quotations from the Targum, is open to question. One would be at a loss to explain the identity of these citations with the rendering in the Targum. For one of the mind of Geiger, who makes the general assertion that citations from the Targumim are not to be found except in the latter Midrashim, it will be of interest the following remark in נבחר מפנינים to Gen. r. 45,7: ודרך המדרש להביא בכמה מקומות את התרגום בפרט בשם מקום מטעם ששם התרגום ההוא היה מפורסם ונודע בעולם יותר. This is just as true of other cases.

6) Com. Field Hex. XVII. Of all the 12 respective citations, one, on Is. 5, 6 (Eccl. r. 11, 7) belongs to Jonathan, and yet carries the name of Aquila. Luria l. c. would emend Jonathan but admits Jonathan is never mentioned in the Midrash. Einhorn (ad loc.) would have here Aquila agree with Jonathan, so Herzfeld (Geschichte II, 63). Equally, Weiss' assertion (Dor, v. 2, 123) that this implies Aquila must have made use of Jonathan needs no refutation. Another Aramaic quotation referring to Prov. 25, 11 (Gen. r. 93, 3) is partly taken from the Targum to Prov.

Yet they are not traced to their respective translators. Such is also the case in Babli, where this tradition of Jonathan's authorship is told. In all the many quotations from Targum Jonathan there is no single reference to Jonathan. These facts combine to show that both in Babylonia and Palestine this tradition was otherwise understood, and not until a com-paratively late period did it succeed in gaining currency.

Aquila's authority, then, in these cases is a mistake. One other case, namely that referring to Lev. 19, 20 (Y. Kid. 1, 1 end) deals with a Halakic exposition. In the first place, it implies in no way a trans-latory interpretation. Further, the authority of Aquila given in the name of Jochanan is contested by Chiya who refers it to R. Laser, changing only the reference for evidence. On the other hand, in the Babli (Krithoth 11b) no authority is cited for the same interpretation. If the authority of Aquila was correctly quoted, then תרגם should be in-terpreted in its general sense as תרגמא is used in the Babli. His trans-lation was not meant, and all assumptions by De Rossi (Meor Einaim, Ch. 45) and Krauss (Steinschneider Fest. 153) in this case deserve little consideration. The case of Dan. 8, 13, where Aquila is cited (Gen. r. 21, 1; Jalqut Dan. l. c.) in Hebrew, is instructive. There can be no question that the words תרגום אנקלס are an interpolation. It is Rab Huna's interpretation played on a particular form of the word and the contracted פלוני : it should read: רב הונא פנייה, לפנימי זה אדה"ר . It admits of no other explanation.

It is not necessary to enlarge upon these four non-Greek citations. It is scarcely necessary to state that none of these citations is to be found in the Hexapla. But of no more valid authenticity are the re-maining eight Greek citations. The citation of Lev. 23, 40 (Y. Sukka 3, 5 Gem.) is a misquotation. As Field and others remarked, such a rendering is fundamentally foreign to Aquila. Besides, in Babli (Sukka 35a) this is recorded as said by Ben Azai, and deducted by the אל תקרי method. In Yerushalmi, again, R. Tanchuma is citing Aquila אמר ר' תנחומא תרג' אנקלוס תרגם אקץ הדר הידור . This is striking. Aquila is always cited plainly. In the Midrash, however (Lev. r. 30, 8; Jalqut l. c.), the name of R. Tanchuma is omitted. At the same time Ben Azai is cited in the Midrash as the authority of the saying הדר זה הדר באילנו משנה לשנה while in Babli l. c. R. Abbahu is mentioned as the author, and in Yerushalmi (l. c.) R. Levi is the one who said it. It appears that Ben Azai's authority was particularly intended for the last part of the saying, namely the citation from Aquila, as if Ben Azai were citing Aquila. A reconciliation of the Babli and Yerushalmi on this point would appear to have been in the view of the compiler. That might have been the case in the Yerushalmi. According to one report, R. Tanchuma was the author of this exegetic note, just as Ben Azai is

Furthermore, Targum Jonathan is quoted in Babli, in many instances, in the name of Rab Joseph, the president of the Pumbeditha Academy, who flourished in the fourth century. Even as late as the author of a commentary on Taharoth, for a long time ascribed to Hai Gaon (flourished in the 11th Century), quotations from Targum Jonathan are given in the name of Rab Joseph, which led Zekaria Frankel, Schürer, Buhl, Winter u. Wünsche, Graetz and many others to take Rab Joseph as the

---

named as its author in the Babli; according to the other, it was Aquila's (interpretation, not translation). And both reports were united in the form it reads in the Yerushalmi. Either B. A. or R. T. made use of the semblance of the respective Hebrew word to the Greek word, a method pursued extensively by the Agadists (Com. Shab. 63b; Gen. ı. 99, 7; com. Shorr תחלוין 12, 6.). It is not Aquila's translation which is quoted. Zipper's Theory (Krauss l. c.) as well as Rappaport's fine sug-gestion (ערך מלין, אתרג) employed by Krauss (l. c. 153) in this case, are superfluous. Of a similar nature is the interpretation attributed to Aquila in Lev. ı. 33, 6 on Ez. 23:43. This curious explanation could hardly have found a place in the literal translation of Aquila. It does not belong to Aquila.

With reference to the allegorical interpretation of Prov. 18:21, attributed in Lev. r. 33, 1 to Aquila, it was justly characterized by Field (l. c.) along with Lev. 23:40 as "Omnino absurdae et ridiculae sunt". Com. Tanchuma Lev. מצורע 4, where practically the same idea is expressed without resorting to this Greek expression.

Questionable is the quotation from Aquila on Ps. 48, 21, cited in Y. Meg. 2, 4; Y. M. K. 3, 7. In the first place, Aquila renders על עלמות Ps. 46, 1 by ἐπίνεανιοτήτων . So a l s o i n 9:1 νειότητος . It stands to reason that 48, 21 was similarly rendered by him and not by the alleged ἀθανασία . This would agree with the T. rendering ביומי טליותנא which is also indicated in the Y. (l. c.), namely בעלימות   It should also be noticed in passing that one other interpretation given there הוא ינהגנו בעולם הזה agrees with the Lxx, which renders it εἰς τοὺς εἰῶνας , which is also i m p l i e d in Cant. r. 1, 22. The Syriac Hex., as well as Jerome (Field XXVI), would lend support to such a rendering by Aquila. The rendering ἀθανασία cited in Field (l. c.) under column Ed. Prima, ought not to be take in serious consideration for obvious reasons. To all intents, this rendering of עלמות is so Midrashic that it would not find its way even into a less rigorous translation than Aq.

The quotation in Y. Shab. 6, 4 from Aq. on Is. 3:20 is not found in the Hex. The case of Ez. 16, 10 (Lam. r. 1, 1), containing a double rendering, may even be a quotation from Jon. The Lxx might as well

real author of the T. Jonathan.[7] But Rashi and Tosaphoth are
unqualifiedly right in their common explanation of this curious
occurrence.[8] It should be borne in mind that Rab Joseph himself often cites the Targum Jonathan with the introductory phrase
אלמלא תרגומא דהאי קרא, which clearly signifies he had the Targum before him.[9] Furthermore, Rab Joseph also cites Onkelos.[10] On the other hand, we have a citation from the Targum
to Esth. 3, 1, ascribed to Rab Joseph, where it is clear from the
Greek names it contains that we have a Palestinian Targum
before us.[11] Again, some of Rab Joseph's interpretations fail to
coincide with those in the Targum Jonathan.[12] In addition,

---

be meant, which here, as also in Ex. 27:16, agrees with Aq. as recorded
in the Hex., and also disagrees, just as Aq., with its version in the
Midrash. Similarly, the citation from Aq. on Gen. 17:1 in Gen. r. 46, 2;
in this case also there is no telling which Greek translation was meant,
for the Lxx contains also such a rendering (com. Field Hex., l. c.). The
ascription, again, to Aq. of citations from other sources was demonstrated
above. This might have been the case with the quotations from Aq. on
Dan. 5, 5 (Y. Joma 3, 8 Gem.) and Esth. 1. 6. In the former, Aq.
is preserved in the Lxx only.

7) Keilim 29, 30 on Judges 3:16; IS. 3:23, 13:21; Ez. 17:7;
Oholoth 18 on Is. 49:22. It is interesting that the Aruch (גלד 2, גמד 2)
cites the Targum from Hai, refraining from mentioning the source, by
the same direct reference to R. Joseph ומתרגם רב יוסף .

Com. Schürer, Geschichte, VI, 149 (4th German ed); Z.
Frankel, Zu d. T., 10-12; Buhl, Kanon, 173; Winter u. Wünsche, Jüd.
Lit. 1, 65.

Winter u. Wünsche, ib., would interpret the tradition as pointing
to the authorship of Jonathan of the fragmentary Targum to the
Prophets in Codex Reuch. Com. also Weiss, Dor, 1, 200; 2, 123.

8) Rashi, Kidushin 13a; Tos. Baba Kama 3a כדמתרגם .

9) San. 94b; Moed Katan 28b; Meg. 3a.

10) Shab. 28a; Exod. 25:5, 64; Num. 31, 50; Nazir 39a; Num.
6:9; Sota 48b: Deut. 1:49, the latter ascribed to Rab Shesheth in
another recension.

11) As to the existence of a Targum to Esther at a comparatively early date, com. Megilla 17a, Mishna and Gemara 18a; Y. Meg.
2, 1. As to the assumption of Rab Joseph being the author of the
Targum to Hagiog., com. Tosafoth Shab. 115a ובידו and Megilla 21b
ובמגילה pointing out that the Targum to Hag. dates back to the
Tanaitic age, while Rashi Megilla (l. c.) עשרה asserts שאין תרגום
בכתובים .

12) Here are some illustrations: Aboda Zara 4a, R. Joseph's in-

in the instance of the Targumic citation on Is. 33:21 put in the mouth of R. Joseph in Jomma 77b, it is given in the name of Rab in Rosh Hashana 23a, and on no authority in Shek. 6, 2, Gem. It may be further stated that in some instances the authority of R. Joseph is omitted; these are introduced by the impersonal דמתרגמינן Again, it should be noticed that Onkelos to Genesis 49:27 and Gen. 30:14 is said in the name of Rab and Levi (Zebachim 54a) רב מתרגם, לוי מתרגם and San. 99b on Gen. 30:14 without מתרג' , and still this would not constitute sufficient evidence to place the name of Rab on Targum Onkelos. The evidence in question presses in the direction of an entirely different conclusion, and that is, that so general was the ignorance of the authorship of the official Targumim that quotations from them were permitted or had to be recalled on the authority of the one citing them.

There is no need to dwell at length on the fanciful hypothesis first formulated by Drusius and later set forth in his peculiar way by Geiger and supported by Karpeles, connecting Jonathan with Theodotion.[13] According to this theory, the Targum Jonathan is founded on the Greek translation of Theodotion, while Targum Onkelos is based on Aquila.[14] But the Theodotion version, which is rather a revised version of the Lxx than an independent rendering, and whose Pharasaic origin is open to question, and whose author shows a scant knowledge of Hebrew, could hardly become the groundwork for the Rabbinic Targum Jonathan. There is not the remotest agreement between them, either as to the principles employed or as to the rendering, except in the names of the translators, and only a

terpretation of Ez. 9:6; Shab. 26a on Jerem. 52:16; Shab. 54b; Kethuboth 6b on IS. 17:8, which involves an Halakic exposition cited also in Shab. 56a. This is contained in the Toseftoic addition on the margin of Codex Reuch. That Rab Joseph, however, was also an independent interpreter appears from his interpretation of Gen. 10, 2 (Joma 10a), in which he disagrees with the extant Targumim, while Ps. Jonathan agrees with R. Simoi (R. Simon in Gen. r. 37, 1).

13) Geiger, Ursch. 163; Carpeles, History (Heb.) 159.

14) Com. Rapaport אגרות לאחרונים זכרון 3; Luzzatto אגרות 214; Adler נתינה לגר Introduction.

highly powerful imagination would be taken by its suggestive-ness.

With the collapse of these theories; with the tradition in complete silence over the name of the author of the official Targum to the Prophets, and in utter lack of other evidence leading to the establishment of a tenable hypothesis, there is no use in further attempts to solve the riddle. There was no single author to impress tradition, and in so far as the name of the author is concerned, the discussion should be considered as concluded. But there is another question closely allied with this problem, which calls for consideration. Many writers on this subject speak of a revised redaction of the official Targumim. Some assert that the revision was stimulated by a missionary desire to supply the Gentile world, speaking an Aramaic dialect, with a correct rendering of the Torah, as Luzzato, supported by Rappaport, would put it.[15] Others would look for its cause in the careless handling by the early Aramaic translators of the Hebrew text.[16] Berliner and Geiger adhere to the theory that the revision was brought about by the necessity of furnishing the congregations in the Diaspora, particularly in Babylonia, with a unified and carefully redacted Aramaic version of the Bible.[17]

It should be first borne in mind that these theories start from the viewpoint that these Targumim were, so to speak, rejected in Palestine and consequently found elevation to general reverence in Bablyonia. This theory of Palestinian disregard for the Targum is already shown to be erroneous. On the whole, however, this theory will, on full examination, prove to be perplexing. The question arises, how is it, that the redactors permitted renderings to remain in the Targum which unmistakably signify a different reading from the Masoretic text? [18]

---

15)   Luzzatto, Oheb, VIII; Rapaport l. c.

16)   Meor Enaim, Ch. 45.

17)   Ur. 164, Nach. Schriften 4, 103; Berliner, On. 108-110. Com. Rapoport אגרות שד"ל p. 214. Weiss, Dor 11, 123; Deutsch in Smith's Dictionary of the Bible 3411. Com. also Jost, Geschichte d. Jud., v. 2, 54, Note 1.

18)   Com. chapter on textual variations, group A.   As to Onk.,

It is further assumed that the revision was made necessary in order to make the Targumic interpretations conform to current Halakic exposition. If this were the case, we should expect to find the Targum in complete harmony with current Halaka. But this is far from being the case. Onkelos presents a long list of cases where it differs from the formally accepted Halakic interpretations and decisions. So are the renderings of Exod. 21, 24 and Lev. 24, 19, 20 against the accepted Halaka, "transmitted from Moses and so seen at the court of every genera-tion from Joshua and on" (Maimonides 1, 6 הלכות חובל ומזיק) that a monetary and not a corporal retaliation is meant (Baba Kama 83b, 84a); Lev. 19:32 disregarding Baraitha Kidushin 32; Deut. 23:18 against Halaka. Sifri l. c.; San. 54b; Abodah Zara 36b. (com. Maimonides הל"א ביאה ב, הל, and יד החזקה איסורי Magid Mishna l. c.). In all of which the Targum undoubtedly has preserved an afterwards superseded Halaka.[19]

The same may be said, in a certain measure, of the Agada. Many are the cases both in Jonathan and Onkelos where the popular interpretations are ignored but which could hardly be ignored by a later redaction.[20] Pseudo-Jonathan and the Frag-

com. Rosenthal in Weiss' Beth Talmud, 2, 284. The adduced evidence, however, tends rather to contradict his hypothesis of a late single com-position of T. Jonathan. Com. also כרם חמד 1, 220.

19) It is instructive to notice the rendering of the respective cases in Ps. Jonathan, which conform with the Halaka. This betrays the hand of a later day editor. The Ps. Jonathan, as is generally known, con-tains some Halakic interpretations conflicting with the current Halaka, which led some writers, among them Geiger, to regard it as a mine of early, Sadducean Halaka. Com. Revel, Karaite Halaka, p. 18.

20) Some examples: Is. 17:8; Kethuboth 9b; Ezek. 1:14; Hagiga 13b; com. also the singular rendering of vv. 5, 6. Com. Hag. l. c.; Kid 72a, referring to 2K 18:11. Both official Targumim abound with such cases.

Yawetz (תולדות ישראל v. 9, 254-264) is the author of a novel theory, namely, that Rab Joseph was the redactor of both Onkelos and Jonathan, as it is evident from the Targumic citations in the Talmud which are quoted in his name. These Targumim have originated from the Greek translation of Aquila, which was translated into Aramaic.

mentary Targum may serve as instructive illustrations. Finally, there are many inconsistencies in reference to certain principles followed in the Targum (com. groups B and C in the chapter on textual deviations), which would not have occurred had it proceeded from the hand of a single redactor. Nothing, again, can account for the silence in the Talmudic sources over an act of such magnitude and importance. The tradition of the Babli of the official Targumim can hardly be taken in any degree to contain the historical kernel of a single authorship. It might be assumed, on the other hand, that it does not, in substance, imply that Jonathan was the author of the extant Targum or of one lost, but points to the fact that this great Rabbi was preeminently skillful in the interpretation of the Prophets. Targum would then be used in this case in its acquired and more general sense. Targum as a quality is counted among the merits of the fellow student of Jonathan, Rabban Jochanan b. Zakkai.[21]

What has been said of Jonathan is true of Onkelos. There could not have been a revised redaction of the magnitude the sponsors of this theory maintained. The corruptionist hypothesis rests on the doubtful foundation that the unofficial Targumim, as Pseudo-Jonathan, to which unfavorable references are supposedly made in the Talmud, preceded the official Targum. But just the reverse may be true, namely, that these extra-Targumim were built upon the official Targum. Suffice it to say that the existence of "Our" Targum, stated by Tanaitic authorities, implies the fact that the other Targumim existed along with the official Targum.

Rab Joseph edited and put them in final shape. Hence the name of Aquila (Onk.) on the Targum of the Pentateuch and also of the Prophets (namely, the citation in Eccl. r. 11, 3 from Jonathan Is. 5:6, which was considered above) and of Rab Joseph on the Targum of the Prophets and also of the Pent. (the citation in Sota 48b). It is the queerest of theories propounded on the question of the authorship of the Targumim. Ingenuity must fail when one identifies the literal Aquila with the interpretative Jonathan.

21)   Soferim 16, 8: אמרו עליו על רבן יוחנן בן זכאי שלא חניח פרשה פרשה, אחת מהתורה שלא למרו במקרא ותרגום מדרש הלכות ואגדות , which is omitted in the modified version of this saying in Sukka 28a and Baba Bathra 134a; so also in אגרת דרב שרירא   Com. also Sifri Deut. 179: למען ילמד ליראה, מלמד שהמורא מביא לידי מקרא, מקרא מביא לידי תרגום תרגום מביא לידי משנה,

But this does not imply that no change was introduced in
the existing official Targumim. Certain traces in the Targum
carry unmistakable evidence of a Babylonian recast, which was,
however, of a very limited scope.

This will be discussed later. The substance was left untouched. Consequently, we may rest assured there was no unified
authorship even to the extent of a thoroughgoing redaction.
But before advancing other views with regard to the authorship,
we might well direct our attention to evidence preserved in
the Targum.

It should be noticed at the outset that tradition assigns an
early origin to the official Targumim. The same tradition which
vaguely ascribed the Targum to late authorities is sponsor of the
statement that they originated far back of the age of these
authorities. Of Jonathan the tradition makes clear that he "said"
the Targum from the mouths of the Prophets Haggai, Zachariah
and Malachi. With regard to Onkelos the tradition explains
that Onkelos only restored the Targum, which originated with
Ezra. The latter was inferred, in the name of Rab, from the
interpretation of Nehemiah 8:8, according to which מפורש
carries the meaning of תרגום (R. Judan, Nedarim 37a; Gen. r.
36, end). Making all allowance, the Targum Jonathan contains
evidence pointing to a comparatively early date. Evidence of a
general character consists, first, of the textual deviations which
abound in Jonathan as well as in Onkelos. [22] The
same may be said with reference to the unacceptable Halaka,
found in Onkelos. This fact points to a date when these matters
were still in the balance. Why, however, they were permitted at
a later age to remain in the Targum can easily be explained.
There was first of all the tradition referring the Targumim to
the last Prophets and Ezra, which cast a halo over them, and
none would venture either to question the propriety of the ren-

22) Rosenfeld's long list of supposed deviations from the M. T.
in Talmud (Mishpachoth Soferim, Vilna, 1883) will be found on closer
examination to present no contradiction to this statement. With minor
exceptions, nearly all the adduced cases are of a Midrashic nature and
should be regarded as such.

dering or attempt to emend them, just because they appeared amazingly striking.

There was no cause for general alarm. The Targum was read verse for verse with the Hebrew Text, which would bring home to the reflection of the hearer the established reading.[23] Still, precaution was sought to exclude a possible impression that the Targum represents the right reading. I am persuaded to interpret the causes for the limitations placed upon the reading of the Targum in the light of this supposition.[24]

The elimination of anthropomorphisms, so persistently carried through in the official Targumim, goes back to an early period. It is a tendency which has its roots in the movement that gave rise to the 18 Tikune Soferim (Mek. Ex. 17, 7) and to the substitution of descriptive appelations (Adonai, Heaven, etc.) for the name of God.[25] In the later part of the Amoraic age a reaction set in against this tendency, which did not reappear until the Arabic Era. This principle would not have been so singularly stressed in the 4th century in Babylonia, not to speak of the 7th century. Numerous anthropomorphic substitutes were eliminated in the official Targumim by the latter redactors, to whom, it would seem, the anthropomorphic expression was no longer terrifying and repugnant.

It will be of some interest in this connection to note the relaxing of this principle in the Targum to Hagiog., which is certainly later than the Targumim to the Pent. and Prophets. This targumist does not hesitate to render literally such expressions as God laughs (Ps. 2:4; 37:13), God sees (Ps. 33:13; 35:17, 22 etc), God's eyes and eyelids (Ps. 11:4; 33:18), God's hands

---

23)   Com. Meg. 23b; Tos. Meg. 3; Rosh Hashana 27a.

24)   Com. Sota 39b and Y. Meg. 4, 1 Gem. The alleged reason שלא יאמרו תרגום כתוב בתורה becomes more sensible if interpreted to mean that the public should not suppose the Targum version to correspond to the established reading.

25)   It was this tendency which influenced both the Aramaic and the Lxx versions. Com. Z. Frankel, Vorstudien, p. 175; Einfluss, pp. 30, 82, 130; Palaest u. Alex. Shrift., 21 et seq.; Zeller, Philosophie d. Griechen, v. 3, 11; 3, 253.

(Ps. 119:73).[26] This reavels the notions of a later generation, which would undoubtedly have come to the surface in the official Targumim, had they been its production.

The term מימרא , employed in the Targumim to cover anthropomorphic expressions, strikes me also as of early origin. It should be noticed at the outset, what a good many have missed to observe, that there is nothing in it to imply Greek influence. It represents no identity. It disavows the slightest implication of an agency. It is merely a term of speech adopted to disguise anthropomorphic presentations, for the awe-inspiring exaltation of God, hiding the face, like Moses, for fear "to look up to God". It was intended not so much to interpret or explain as to remind and evoke a higher reaction. It is fully employed in the same sense as דבר or מאמר is used in the Bible, in which image מימרא was certainly cast.[27] In a later age, under the influence, it would seem, of the Greek Logos, this term acquired the meaning of a definite essence, an embodied heavenly power approaching an intermediary agency.[28] The דבור calls to Moses;[29] it visits, surrounds and kisses.[30] In the Book of Wisdom, probably of Palestinian origin, the all-powerful word of God leaps down from heaven, "a stern warrior into the midst

---

26) L. Ginsburg in the Jewish En. Anthropo. seemingly failed to take notice of this distinction when he made the unqualified statement that the earlier Targumim retained in translation such expressions as the hand, finger, eye etc. of God. This is true of the Targum to the Hagiog. only. In Jonathan an evasive substitute is always employed in such cases. As to the hand of God, com. Joshua 22:31; 1S 5:7; 1K 18:46: Is. 5:25, 9:11, 11:11, 15:31, 3; Jer. 1:9 etc. As to finger, com. Exod. 8:15 with the exceptions of Exod. 31:18 and its parallel in Deut. 9:10, in which case, it seems, the substitute was eliminated, as in the creation story, in order to avoid an explanation that the tablets were given by some inferior power, or to escape the danger of allegorizing the fact of the tablets. Com. further Exod. 33:12, 13; 1 Kings 8:29; Is. 1:15; 43:4; Jer. 7:30.

27) In Ps. 33:6, 9; 107:20; 147:15, 18; 148:8 דבר is a descriptive term for the action of God, while in 119:89 it is descriptive of the Torah.

28) Com. Gen. i. 4, 2.

29) Lev. r. 1, 4.

30) Cant. r. 1:13.

of a doomed land".[31] The term מימרא , then, could not have originated in a period when it might be taken to signify a distinct God-like power. In its use in translation it would have the effect of investing the מימרא with all activity, God being inactive— and nothing could be more horrible to the non-Hellenistic Jew than a transcendentalism of the Alexandrian mould. As was noticed before, the later Bablyonian redactors have limited in the Targum the use of the מימרא   It is remarkable that in the creation story all anthropomorphic expressions are, contrary to principle, literally rendered. In most of the parallel cases in Ps. Jonathan מימרא is inserted. The reason for that might be found in the new significance which this term had assumed, so that the application of this term in the creation story would carry the implication that some other power, separate from God, was the author of the act of the creation.[32]

The Targum to the Prophets is not wanting in more specific evidence, although this sort of evidence is admittedly scant. This T. is far from being Midrashic. It is primarily a translation, and the chief concern of the translator is to find the right mean-ing and the interpretation of the word and phrase; it is not seeking to explain the exigencies of the age, or to propound the mysteries of the generations. It does, however, in a few cases make use of allegory. In the allegorical interpretation un-mistakable allusions were preserved to events which can be placed. The events extend over many periods, which furnish us the clue to the historical origination of the Targum.

Direct historical reference is made in the Targum to Hab. 3:17:   כי תאנה לא תפרח ואין יבול בגפנים, כחש מעשה זית... The Targum interprets this to refer to the four Kingdoms ארבע מלכיות [33] But referring to Rome, the version reads ישתיצון רומאי

31) Wisdom 18:15. Com. also 16:12; 4 Esd. 6:38.

32) Com. On. Gen. 3:9, 22; 5:2; 6:3. In all these cases Ps. Jonathan has מימרא inserted. In Gen. 8:1 there is a complete agreement in the translation between On. and Ps. Jonathan, except that the latter has מומרא . No explanation can plausibly account for that, except the supposition that a later redactor, out of fear for a possible misleading in-ference, and who would not feel irritated over an anthropomorphic expression, eliminated מומרא in the respective cases.

33) The reading of the extant editions ומזלות כוכבים עובדי וגברי

ולא יגבון קיסומא מירושלם. This emphasis on the tribute by the targumist is remarkable. None of the barbarities committed by
the Romans inflamed his rage as did the tribute. This reference
then, must have been coined at a time when the chief agitation
of the people gathered around the problem of the tribute. The
targumist meant the census instituted by the second Procurator
Quirinius (6-7 C. E.), which aroused rebellion, being regarded
by the people as bondage. Had the destruction of the Temple
taken place at the time of this reference to Rome, this act would
have certainly been recorded instead of the census.[34]

IS. 28:1: הוי עטרת גאות שכורי אפרים... translating allegorically:
וי די יהיב כתרא לגיותנא טפשא רבה דישראל ויהיב מצנפתא לרשיעיא
רבית מקדש תושבחתיה. In the same way also vv. 3, 4. Allusions are
here made to the deplorable state of the High Priesthood. The
reference may go to the Sadducean Hasmonean rulers, particularly
to Alexander Jannaeus, who incurred the deadliest hatred of the
people. This hatred of the "sinners who rose against us"; who
"laid waste the throne of David in tumultous arrogance" (Ps.
of Sol. 17, 4-8); who "utterly polluted the holy things of the
Lord (1, 8) and had profaned with iniquities the offerings of
God" (2, 3).[35] Reference to John Hyrcanus is made in Ps.
Jonathan to Deut. 33:11, according to Geiger (Ur. 479), which,
however, may also be equally applicable to the father of Mattath-
ias, John, whom later authorities, mistakenly, took for a High
Priest. The failure, however, of the targumist to allude to the
Kingship of the sinful High Priest, speaks against this supposition. It is a safer supposition that the Herodian High Priests
or the state of the High Priesthood under the Roman Procurators,
when this most sacred dignity became a salable article, is here

---

is a later emendation, probably to escape the rigors of the censor. It
should read with Lagarde, גברי יון .

34) Com. Ant. XVII. 21. As to the date of the Census, com.
Schürer, Geschichte, 4th German ed. VI, erste Anhang. Com. also
Hausrath N. T. Times (Eng. ed.) v. 2, pp. 74-83. It was this state
of mind from which emanated the curious rendering of והמכשלה
(Is. 3:6) ומגביתא , taxation, against the Agadic interpretation to mean
the Law (Chag. 14b; Gittin 43b). Com also Is. 55:5.

35) Com. also 8:10, 13, 26. Com. Buchanan, Charles, Apocrypha.
II, 628.

meant.[36] I am persuaded to believe that the targumist had in mind particularly the appointment by Herod of Annanel to the High Priesthood, which by right and general expectation was to belong to Aristobul III.[37]

IS. 64:11: העל אלה תתאפק is so rendered as to give vent to the general excitement of the time. It runs: העל אלין תתחסן ואת יהיב ארכא לרשיעיא דמישעבדין בנא עד עלמא ; likewise Hab. 3:1. The wicked are the rulers over the people. They are not the Gentiles, Romans, whom the T. would call either by name or by the general appelation עממיא, גוים ; ודשיעיא is applied to the wicked of Israel only. I am inclined to think the allusion is made to the Herodian rulers rather than to the later Hasmo-nean rulers. The expression ואת יהיב ארכא could hardly have been intended for Alexander Jannaeus, whose rule was not too long, being then followed by the just rule of Alexandra. The targumist would, at the same time, place the beginning of the Herodian rule in the early days of the Antipater's political as-cendency. There are other references to the Herodian rulers.

Hos. 4:13 על כן תזנינה בנותיכם is rendered על כן מזנין בנתכון דהואה לכון מבנת עממיא וכלתכון דנסבתון לבניכון מן עממיא גיפן.

---

36) Com. Ant. XX, 8, 8; Pesachim 57a; Tos. Menachoth end.
אוי לי מבית ביתוס, אוי לי מאלתם. אוי לי מבית חנין, אוי לי מלחישתם, אוי לי מבית פתרום. אוי לי מקולמוסם ; אוי לי מבית ישמעאל בן פאדי. אוי לי מאגרופם שהם כהנים גדולים ובניהם וחתניהם אמרכלים ועבדיהם חובטים את העם במקלות.
Also Lev. ı. 21, 5; Y. Yoma 1, 1:
... אלא מקדש ראשון שעל ידי ששמשו באמונה שמשו בו י"ח כהנים, מקדש שני על שהיו נוטלין אותה בממון וי"א שהיו הורגין זה את זה בכשפים שמשו פ' כהנים, ומהן שמעון הצדיק מ' שנה. ביון שחזרו להיות משכירין אותו בדמים היו שנותיהן מתקצרות. מעשה באחד ששלח ביד בנו שתי מדות של כסף... ועמד אחד ושלח ביד בנו שתי מדות של זהב... אמרו כפה סיח את המנורה. Com. Yoma 9a.

37) Ant. XV, 2, 4. This reference might also be applicable to the High Priest Simon the son of Boethus, whose daughter Herod loved and married, and, in order to augment the dignity of the family, con-ferred upon him this high honor (Ant. XV, 9, 3). Although a priest of note, his elevation to office in this manner and the overthrow of Jesus the son of Phabet, his predecessor, brought upon him the indigna-tion of the people and the hatred they entertained for the Herodian dynasty.

This is certainly an early T.; v. 14 is interpreted literally. Had it been the intention of the T. to soften some harsh ex-pression flung against the morality of the Jewish daughters, it would have been followed in the other v. But the former deals a rebuke to the Herodians, who have intermarried with Gentile rulers. Herod married a Samaritan woman (Ant. 12, 2, 19); his son Alexander—Glaphira, daughter of Archelaus, King of Cappadocia (Ant. 16, 1, 2); Drusilla, the sister of Agrippa II, was prevailed upon to transgress the laws of her forebears and to marry Felix, the procurator (Ant. 20, 7, 2), while her former husband, the heathen King of Emesa and the second husband of her sister Berenice, the King of Cilicia, though circumcised, would hardly be regarded as a proselyte. The latter renounced his conversion as soon as Berenice left him (Ant. ib.). The cohabi-tation of Berenice with Titus (Dio Cassius 66, 15) is a further instance. It was the general reaction towards this open violation of the Law which the Rabbi would express in the only safe way through the exposition of some Prophetic utterance.

Of a more pronounced nature is the reference contained in the T. to Is. 65:4 דיתבן בבתיא — הישבים בקברים ובנצורים ילינו רבנן מעפר קבריא ועם פגרי בני אנשא דירין . It is a valuable historical statement of the erection of Tiberias. Herod Antipas built it on a site strewn with sepulchres. This was resented by the ortho-dox Jews, who would not, on account of uncleanliness, settle there, even after the sepulchres had been removed. Herod was on that account impelled to bring pressure to bear on the first settlers, a great many of whom were strangers, poor people and slaves. (Com. Ant. 18, 2, 3; Gen. r. 23, 1). The whole incident was soon to be forgotten, as the city came to assume great emi-nence in the Great Rebellion, although the more scrupulous would still hesitate, until the time of R. Simon Ben Jochai (com. Shab. 34a) to settle in certain parts of it. So that this indignation of the targumist must emanate from the very time of the act of Herod. This T. belongs to 28 C. E.

I am inclined to think that the T. to Am. 6:1 נקבי ראשית מקימין שום בניהון כשום בני עממי — הגוים refers to the Herodians and their followers, who would give themselves foreign names, and were not known, like the Hasmoneans, by the Hebrew double. As it is well known, Jews during the Hasmonean rule

would unhesitatingly give themselves Greek names. But this
practice grew abominable in the sentiment of the people in the
days of the Herodian rulers. There are many references to
this effect in the Agada (Exod. r. 1, 30; Lev. r. 32, 3; Tan.
Balak 25, etc.), all of which, I suppose, emanated from that
period. Com. also Hos. 8:12.

The reference in T. to Ez. 39:16 to the destruction of Rome
is interesting. It suggests that the T. took Rome as גוג. As Gog
is the Messianic foe of Israel, one feels that in the time of
either the Great or the Bar-Kochba Rebellion, the revolutio-
naries, in their pious and Messianic mood, would take Rome as
the prophetic גוג , so that its overthrow is sure to come. Hence
the source of the targumic interpretation. I am also led to believe that this was the reason why the T. turns the gloomy and
miserable description of the "Servant" (Is. ch. 53) into a most
glorious presentation. The targumist, living in a time when the
Messiah stood at the head of warring armies, could hardly have
conceived those objectionable features in a literal sense. V. 5
points clearly to Bar Kochba.

והכרתי סוסיך מקרבך והאבדתי מרכבתיך... 12 ,10 ,5:9 .Mi
והכרתי ערי ארצך והרסתי כל מבצריך... והכרתי פסיליך ומצבותיך מקרבך.
The T. changes the simple meaning of the words and renders
them this way:

ואשיצי סוסות עממיא מבינך ואוכיד רתיכיהון (9). ואשיצי קרוי עממיא
מארעך ואפגיר כל כרכיהון תקיפיא (10). ואשיצי צלמי עממיא וקמתהון
מבינך (12) .

This is a curious rendering. The second half of v. 12 is rendered literally. All other references in the Prophets to the
idolatry of Israel are rendered literally by the T. But the T. in
these verses is construed to give expression to the popular resentment of the act of Herod to construct heathen cities in
Palestine, and the erection in them of temples and statues.

Another allusion to a contemporary situation is found in
the Targum to Judges 5:11. The interpretation reads: מאתר רהון
אנסין להון ונסבין דבידיהון בית מכונת לסטין ומתובת מוכסין . There
is here the twofold reference to the robber and to the publican.
In both aspects the hint is to the last days of Jerusalem. The ab-

horrence for the publican, who was considered an outlaw,[38] was general among the people in those troublesome days. Regarding the former, the implication seems to be of the activities of the Sicarii under the Procuratorship of Felix or Festus, particularly the latter, of whom Josephus says that·upon his coming Judea was afflicted by robbers while all the villas were set on fire and plundered by them.[39] The targumist is setting the mark on the facts against which his generation most vehemently reacted.

The interpretation of the T. of ויפקדם בטלאים (Is. 15:4) ומנינין באמרי פסחא is also suggestive of an event preceding the destruction of the Temple which is told in the Talmud of Agrippa I, that wishing to know the number of the people while avoiding its prohibition, he asked the High Priest to count the Paschal sacrifices.[40] I would not, however, stress this evidence. A later targumist might as well have used for exegetical purpose a current Agada.

Of more historical suggestiveness is the Targum to Ze. 11, 1 פתח לבנון דלתיך interpreted to refer to the heathen peoples and the destruction of their cities. This verse was interpreted by Rabban Jochanan b. Zakkai to imply the pending destruction of the Temple, which was generally accepted. [41] Why a targumist living in a generation impressed by the destruction of the Temple should select so strange an allegorical interpretation is hardly conceivable. It would seem that he did not know of the destruction of the Temple and was imbued with the political Messianism, which was an important factor in the Rebellions.

The Targum, however, also contains evidence pointing to a period subsequent to the destruction of Jerusalem. Is. 54:1

---

38) Com. B. Kama 113a, Mish.; Shab. 39a; San. 25b.

39) Ant. XX, 9, 10. The distinction should be drawn between the patriots and the sicarii who, to all intents, were robbers of the vilest sort and employed by Felix for the purpose of inflaming unrest to screen his outrages.

40) Pesachim 64b; Tosefta 4. Com. Wars 6, 9, 3. There are strong reasons for assuming that it was a historical reality.

41) עד שגער בו, רבן יוחנן בן זכאי אמר לו : היכל היכל מפנימה אתה מבעית עצמך, יודע אני שסופך עתיד ליחרב וכבר נתנבא עליך זכריה בן עדוא פתח לבנון וכ"ו. Yoma 39b, and in Yerushalmi in a somewhat modified version, 6, 3 end.

ארי סגי יהון the Targum interprets כי רבים בני שוממה מבני בעולה בני ירושלים צדיתא מבני רומה יתבתא.

In the same sense Is. 2:5 עד עקרה ילדה שבעה ורבת בנים אמללה is rendered in the Targum כן ירושלים דהות כאתתא עקרא עתידה דתתמליא מעם גלותהא ורומי דמליא סגי עממיא יסופון . Jerusalem is here seen to be desolate. Rome is in its bloom. There is still the thirst for revenge from Rome, which also found expression in the Targum to Is. 25:12 meaning by כרך Rome, and Ez. 39:16. Com. also Targum Is. 32:14. The targumist lived in a period following the destruction but not too far away. Mi. 7:11 is interpreted in the T. to refer to the cessation of the persecutions of the nations: בערנא ההיא יתבטלן גזירת עממיא . The reference is to the situation which arose in Palestine after the rebellion of Bar Kochba. The targumist had in mind the persecutions of Hadrian. It is hardly appropriate to the political repressions of the Roman Procurators. It might be well applied to the persecutions of the Byzantine rulers which, however, could hardly have found room in the Palestinian Targum, known and used in Babylonia in the third century.

A less pronounced indication of a post-Destruction age is suggested in the T· to Malachi 1:11 ובכל מקום מקטר מגש לשמי ובכל עירן דאתון עבדין רעיתי אנא אקבל צלותכון... וצלותכון rendering: כקורבן דכי קדמי.

The conception implied here that the prayer replaced the sacrifice is an outgrowth of the age following the destruction of the Temple, after the cessation of sacrifice. The sacrifice was regarded with so much holy reverence by the Rabbis, that such a conception would be considered an attempt at the divinity of the sacrifice.[42]

Finally, the Targum to Is. 21:9 may also be of historical contents. Here the Targum reads נפלת אף עתידא למפל בבל . The wish is here expressed for the downfall of Babylonia. This suggests an age of persecution in Babylonia against the Jews.

---

42) This conception has its origin in the saying of R. Jochanan B. Zakkai: יש לנו כפרה אחת שהיא כמותה (Aboth of R. N. 4, 5). Com. saying of R. Shmuel b. Nachmani on this verse זוהי תפלת המנחה (Jalqut l. c.). So saying of R. Eliezer גדולה התפלה יותר מהקרבנות (Berak. 32b). Com. Jalqut Eliezer קרב : מק אדם אמרו ישראל רבש״ע בזמן שבה״מק מביא קרבן ומתכפר עכשיו אין בידינו אלא תפלת.

Babylonia in an earlier period was looked upon with admiration by the Jews. It was only after the fanatical Sassanides had established themselves on the throne of Persia that the large Jewish population of Babylonia began to experience the same tribulation which their brethren in Palestine were undergoing under the Roman rule.[43] After the new departure in the ruling dynasty, Babylonia, like Rome, incurred the bitter resentment of the Jews. Before the Chebarin (Magii) came to Babylonia, we are told in Gittin 17a, the saying of R. Chiya: "God knew that Israel could not bear the persecution of the Edomites, so he led them to Babylonia" was true, but after their arrival Rabbi Bar Bar Chana was right in his utterance: רחמנא או בטולא דידך און בטולא רבר עשי . This period is implied in the Targum to Is. 28:20 ושלטון בבלאי מעיק — והמסכה צרה כהתכנס יסגי מרוא.

On the other hand, the fall of Babylonia is with the author still a desire, a fervent expectation. The overthrow of Babylonia by the Arabians is not yet in sight. There is no other allusion in the Targum to the Arabs. So that this allusion to Babylonia affords us a terminus ad quem.

To check up the findings, the scant evidence preserved in the Targum to the Prophets falls apart in different groups. Some

43) Com. Saying of Rab. עתידה פרס שתפל ביד רומי Yoma 17a; also Pesachim 54a: תנו רבנן שבעה דברים מכוסים מבני אדם... ומלכות פרס מתי תפול . There is a striking parallel interpretation in Ps. Jonathan Gen. 15:12 referring נפלת to Persia: דעתידא למיפל ולית לה זקיפא ומחמן... or in the version of the Frag. דחא היא מלכותא דפרסיא דעתידא למפל ולא תהווי לה תקומה לעלמי עלמין . It should be remarked that Ps. Jonathan introduces here the Messianic conception of the Four Kingdoms of the Exile, the Fourth being Edom or Rome. The targumist in this instance dismisses Rome, placing in its stead Persia-Babylonia. In the Midrash (Gen. ı. 44, 2), on which this interpretation is based, נפלת is referred to Edom with the parenthetic note: ויש שמחלפין נופלת עליו זו בבל דכתיבה בה נפלה נפלה בבל It is clear that both in the Midrash and the Ps. Jon. Babylonia (or Persia) had come to be regarded as worse than Rome, as fully expressed in the saying of Rab. At the same time, it is made clear in the Midrash that the interpretation of נפלת as referring to Bablyonia is based upon Is. 21:9, consequently the Targum to Is. 21:9 was either known to them and used by the Ps. targumist or that the interpretation in the respective cases was simultanously originated. The former assumption, however, is the more plausible one.

are pointing to a pre-Destruction date, some to a period immediately following the Destruction, some, again, to a still later period. But they do not lead to contradicting results. The evidence demonstrates in a most excellent manner the progressive composition of the Targum until it assumed its present form. During this long time, the Targum was submitted to changes of different natures, when finally, before the Arabic invasion of Babylonia, it was indorsed in the shape in which it has come down to us.

We shall now devote our attention to a study of the relation between the official Targumim. There is a conspicuous affinity between Onkelos and Jonathan. Most of the early writers on this subject were struck by it but failed to realize its extent, which consequently lead them to different conclusions. So, while De Rossi and Herzfeld were certain that Onkelos knew the Targum to the Prophets, Zunz took the view that Jonathan had Onkelos before him, whom he quoted in Judges 5:26; 2 Kings 14:6; Jerem. 48:46.[44] Herzfeld would consider all these citations as later interpolations.[45] But on closer study of the official Targumim the cases of agreements between them will be found to be so numerous and of such a nature that they can be explained neither on the hypothesis of interpolation nor on the assumption of one having made use of the other. The reader will first be referred to the chapter on general peculiarities of Jonathan. The peculiar treatment by this T. of certain expressions, to distinguish between the holy and profane; Israel and other peoples; the belief in a second death for the wicked, all are found in Onk. Besides, there are numerous other cases in which both Targumim agree. I will cite here the Ps. Jonathan only to show that there could be a different rendering in the respective cases.

Josh. 1:6 חזק ואמץ Targum תקף ואלים. So Onkelos Deut. 31:7. Ps. Jon. איתוקף ואתחייל.

ib. 1:9 אל תחת Targum תתבר So Onk. Deut. 31:8. Ps. Jon. תתירע.

44) De Rossi Meor Enaim l. c.; Herzfeld, Geschichte l. c.; Zunz, G. V. l. c.

45) L. c.

ib. 3:13 ...נד ויעמדו Targum רוקבא So Onk. of חמת מים
(Gen. 21:14, 15, 19). Ps. Jon זיקין דמיא. In Exod. 15:8
נצבו כמו נד Onk. קמו כשיר. Ps. Jon. זיקא. The Targum to
Psalms 33:7; 78:13 is זיקא

ib. 7:21 שנער ארדת Targum אצטלי דבבלי. So Onk. Gen.
14:1. Ps. Jon. פונטום.

ib. 10:26 עצים חמשה על ויתלם Targum צליבתא. So Onk.
Lev. 40:19; Deut. 21:22, 23. Ps. Jon. קיסא.

ib. 12:5; 13:13 והמעכתי Targum ואפיקורום. So Onk. Deut.
3:14. Ps. Jon. אנטיקירום [46].

ib. 13:3 הוא ישראל אלהי יהוה נחלה, משה נתן לא לוי ולשבט.
Also נחלתם אחסנתהון ישראל יי להון יהב די מתנן Targum
Ezek. 44:28 אחזתם אני ביישראל להם תתנו לא ואחזה Targum
אחסנתהון אינון להון דיהבית מתנן This is the rendering by Onk.
of Deut. 18:2 נחלתו הוא ה'. But Ps. Jon. מוהבותא וארבע עשרים
דכהונתא.

ib. 14:4 ומגרשיהם Targum ורוחיהון. Also Ezek. 45:2; 48:17.
So Onk. Lev. 25:34; Num. 35:2, 3, 4. Ps. Jon. פרולין.

ib. 20:1 מקלט ערי Targum שיזבותא קרוי. So Onk. Num.
35:6, 11, 13. Ps. Jon. דקטלן קרוי.

ib. 20:5, 9 הדם גאל Targum דמא גאל. So Onk. Num.
35:19, 21, 24, 25; Deut. 19:6. But Ps. Jon. דמא תבע.

ib. 20:5 דעת בבלי כי Targum מדעיה בלא ארי. So Onk.
Deut. 19:4. Ps. Jon. מתכוין בלא.

ib. 23:16 ...מהרה ואברתם ארעא מעל בפריע ותובדון Targum
ומבדון בסרהוביא מעילוי. So Onk. Deut. 11:17. Ps. Jon. טבתא
משבחא ארעא.

Judges 5:8 חדשים אלהים לו יבחר Targum בני אתריעו כר
אבהתהון בהון איתעסקו דלא עבידא דמקרב חדתן לטעותא למפלח ישראל
Onk. to Deut. 32:17 ...באו מקרוב חדשים ידעום לא אלהים Render-
ing: חדתנין אבהתכון בהון איתעסקו לא דמעבידו דמקריב חדתן דחלן
Com. מן כדון אתברון ולא אידכרו בהון אבהתכון Fragmentary
Sifri l. c. and Friedmann On. and Ak., p. 65.

1S. 13:12 ואתאפק Targum ואתחסנית. So Onk. Gen. 45,1.
Ps. Jon. למסוברא.

46) Kohut's suggestion on these renderings (Aruch אפקירום)
will only serve the point in question.

ib. 15:7 שור Targum חגרא. So Onk. Gen. 25:18. Ps. Jon. חלוצה. [47]

ib. 23:22 והכינו Targum ואתקינו. So Onk. Exod. 16:4. Ps. Jon. ואתברדו—ל"א. ויזמנון. [47]

1K. 18:28; 5:16 ויתגדדו Targum ואתחממו. Also Jerem. 47:15. So Onk. Deut. 14:1. Ps. Jon. לא תגודון בשריכין.

2K. 5:16 ויפצר בו Targum ואתקיף ביה. So Onk. Gen. 19:3. Ps. Jon. פיים.

ib. 5:19 כברת ארץ Targum כרוב ארעאי. So Onk. Gen. 35:16; 48:7. Ps. Jon in former: סיגעי אישון עללתא בארבע in latter: סיגעי ארעא.

ib. 6:18 ויכם בסנורים Targum בשברירא. So Onk. Gen. 19:11. Ps. Jon. בחוורדורייא. Frag. בהדבריה.

ib. 16:6 וינשל Targum ותריך. So Onk. Deut. 7:22. Ps. Jon. וינלי.

ib. 18:32 ארץ זית ודבש Targum ארעא דזיתהא עבדין משחא ומן תומרייתא עבדין דבש So Onk. Deut. 8:8. Ps. Jon והיא עבדא דבש דבש.

ib. 21:6 ועונן ונחש ועשה אוב וידענים Targum ועגין ונחיש ועבד So Onk. Lev. 19:26; 20:6; Deut. 18:10, 14. בידין וזכירן Ps. Jon. אחידי עגין.

ib. 23:25 ובכל נכסותי Targum ובכל מאדו. So Onk. Deut. 6:5. Ps. Jon. בכל ממונכון.

IS. 3:20 הצעדות Targum ושירי רגליא. So Onk. Num. 31:50 קדישיא מן אודניהון Ps. Jon. שירין.

Jerem. 7:24 etc. בשררות לבם Targum בהרהור לבהון. So Onk. Deut. 29:18. Ps. Jon. בתהות יצרא ביש.

Ezek. 12:7, 8, 12 עלטה Targum קבלא. So Onk. Gen. 15:17. Ps. Jon. חומטא. Gen. r. 45, 9 אמיטתא.

---

47) Ps. Jon. agrees with On. and Jon. in Gen. 16:7; 20:1. Onkelos renders בין רקם ובין חגרא (ibid 16:14) בין קדש ובין ברד presumably influenced by 20:1 בין קדש ובין שור. Cases of this sort are numerous in Onkelos. Similar cases in Jonathan are cited in the chapter on textual deviations. But as to Ps. Jon., the rendering also of שור in 16:7; 20:1 was חלוצה as in 28:18, in which the Fragmentary concurs. Evidence for this is presented in Gen. r. 45, 9: על עין המים, באורה דחלוצה. Also Ps. Jon. to Exod. 15:22. Gronemann's (Pent. Über., p. 20) argument on this is thus a miscalculation.

לא תחלון‎ Targum ‏ואת שם קדישי לא תחללו עוד‎ ib. 20:39
So Onk. Exod. 20:22; Lev. 21:6, 12, 15; 22:32. Ps. Jon. ‏תפסון‎
But ‏ואחילו‎ (Jer. 31:4) ‏נטעו נטעים וחללו‎. So Onk. Deut. 20:6.
Ps. Jon. ‏פרקיה‎.

ib. 28:13   ‏אדם פטדה ויהלם תרשייט שהם וישפה‎ Targum
‏כמקן ירקן וסבהלם כרום ימא וכורלא ובנתירון שביזי אזמרגדין‎ .So Onk
Exod. 28:17, 18, 19, 20. But not so Ps. Jon. and F.

‏מרחיק רגז ומסגי למעבד‎ Targum ‏ארך אפים ורב חסד‎ Joel 2:13
‏ארך רוח... חסד‎ Ps. Jon. ‏טבון‎ . So Onk. Exod. 34:6.

These cases are of special interest also for determining the
nature of the relation between Onkelos and the non-official Targumim. But of equal importance are the cases of agreement
between the official Targumim in which the non-official Targumim
concur. They also belong to Onkelos. I do not intend to raise
the question of the origin and history of the non-official Targumim to the Pentateuch. I have my own view of them, differing appreciably from those offered. But whether we assume
with Bacher that in the Fragmentary is preserved a relic of the
ancient and original Palestinian Targum on which were based
both Onkelos and Ps. Jonathan which form stages of the same
Targum,[49] or whether we choose the simpler view enunciated
by Traub u. Seligson, that Ps. Jon. and the Fragmentary are
to some extent a critical revision of Onkelos,[50] there is the
general recognition of the common ground of these Targumim
and Onkelos. The fact, therefore, that they agree with Onkelos
cannot be construed to impart to the cases in question a different
character.

Josh. 10:11; 14:6, 7 ‏מקדש ברנע‎ Targum ‏רקם גיאה‎ So Onk.
and Ps. Jon. Num. 32:8 etc.

ib. 12:2 ‏ועד היבק‎ Targum ‏יובקא‎. So Onk. and Ps. Jon. Gen.
32:23; Num. 21:24 etc.

48) This is true only when it is spoken of profanation of God
(Is. 48:11; Ez. 20:9, 14; 22:36; 27:33); profanation of the Sabbath
(Is. 56:2, 6; Ez. 20:16, 21, 24, 38). But when it is spoken of pro-
fanation of the land and temple ‏אפא‎ is employed.

49) Z. D. M. G., v. 28, 60-63.

50) Frankel's Monatschrift, 1857, 101 et seq. Gronemann (Pent.
Übersetz., p. 8, note) also thinks that the Fragmentary and Ps. Jon.,
especially the latter, have expanded Onkelos.

ib. 11:2; 12:3 כנרות Targum גינוסר . So Onk. and Ps. Jon.
Num. 34:11 etc.

ib. 12:8; 10:13, 20 אשדות Targum מישפך מרמתא . So Onk.
and Ps. Jon. Deut. 4:49.

Judges 1:6 ובני קיני Targum ובני שלמאה . So Onk. and
Ps. Jon. Gen. 15:19 and Frag. Num. 24:21, 22.

ib. 3:8 ארם נהרים Targum ארם די על פרת . So Onk. and
Ps. Jon. Gen. 24:10.

ib. 17:5, 12 וימלא את יד Targum וקריב ית קרבן . So Onk.
and Ps. Jon. Exod. 28:41.

1S 19:13, 16 תרפים Targum צלמניא . So Onk. and Ps. Jon.
Gen. 31: 19, 34, 35.

2S 1:19 הצבי ישראל Targum אתעתדון . So On. Exod. 33:21
ותתעתד — ונצבת . Ps. Jon. ותהי מעתד . Also Deut. 29:9.

1K 11:36; 15:4 למען היות ניר Targum מלכו . So Onk. and
Ps. Jon. Num. 21:30 ונירם .

2K 3:13 ...ויאמר למלך ישראל אל Targum בבעו . So Onk. and
Ps. Jon. Gen. 19:7, 18.

ib. 5:21 ויפל מעל המרכבה Targum ואתרכין . So Onk. and
Ps. Jon. Gen. 24:64.

ib. 19:37 ארץ אררט Targum לארעא קרדו . So Onk. and Ps.
Jon. Gen. 8:4. (Ps. Jon. דקדרון) [51] .

There is also agreement between them with regard to the
belief in a second death for the wicked in the Messianic Age.
So Jon. Is. 65:6; Jerem. 51:39. Both Onk. and Frag. render
Deut. 33:6 יחי ראובן בחיי עלמא ומותא תנינא — יחי ראובן ואל ימת
יחי ראובן בעלמא ולא ימות במותנא תנינא דבה ; Frag.: לא ימות
ימין ושמאל . מיתי רשיעיא indicating direction (Is. 9:19; Ezek.
21:21; Zech. 12:6) are rendered by דרומא צפונא . So Onk. and
Ps. Jon. Gen. 13:9. Is. 14:9 רפאים Targum גברין . So Onk.
and Ps. Jon. Gen. 15:20. Chayjoth in אגרת בקרת [52] has brought
to notice the remarkable change in the rendering of עברים
by Onk. Everywhere in Gen. it is rendered עבראי but beginning
with Exod. יהודאי is the rendering. The motive for that might
be the exegetical saying of R. Simeon b. Jochai on Gen. 49:8:

---

51) Cited also in Gen. r. 33, 2.

52) Page 8.

אמר ר׳ שמעון בן יוחאי יהיו כל אחיך נקראין על ישמך, אין אדם אומר
ראובני אנא, שמעוני אנא אלא יהודי אנא.

In that Ps. Jon., with a single exception, agrees. (Gen.
43:32). But Exod. 21:2 כי תקנה עבד עברי and Deut. 15:20; 13:12
כי ימכר לך אחיך העברי או העבריה both Onk. and Ps. Jon. have
בר ישראל in order, it would appear, to avoid the misinterpretation: the slave of an Israelite (com. Mechilta l. c.). Jonathan as
a rule renders יהודאי — עברים 1S 13:3, 17; 14:11, 21; Jonah
1, 9. But Jerem. 34:9 (also 14) לשלח איש את עבדו ואיש את שפחתו
העברי והעבריה. The T. follows Onk. and Ps. Jon. rendering
לשלחא בר ישראל ובת ישראל.

Zech. 12:8 ובית דויד כאלהים Targum כרברבין. So Onk. and
Ps. Jon. Gen. 6:4 בני האלהים — רברביא.

This comparative list could be extended appreciably. But
the number of cases presented are sufficient to show the real
nature of the problem. There could be found sound explanation for the similarity between Onk. and the Frag. and
Ps. Jon. even were we not to proceed along the lines of the
theories offered, for they are exploiting the same field, the Pentateuch. Why, however, should an author of a Targum to the
Prophets seek harmony with Onkelos in many comparatively un-
important details of rendering, will hardly be possible to explain.
Could not the Targum to the Prophets have its own way of
rendering in the respective cases? Neither could it be the way of
a redactor. But this Targum, like the Mishna, Tosefta, Talmudim
and Midrashim, had no single author: there was no single revision. The inference will yield the only possible conclusion
that **there was a common source for the official Targumim. They
were originated in one and the same time; in one and the same
way, under one and the same circumstances and share a common history.**
They were the product of the Aramaic rendering of the
portion from the Law and the Prophets read in public worship.
The Lxx had a similar origination, although later generations, actuated by propaganda motives, formed a different notion
of the act.[53] The official Targumim are the work of genera-

---

53) This view is held by most scholars. "Sie verdanken nicht
der Wissenschaft sondern dem Relig. Bedürfnisse" (Frankel, Vorstudien,

tions. They were formed and reformed through many centuries, gradually, invisibly. They were not a new attempt, supplanted none, but are the continuation of the Targumim used in the service.

Hence also the remarkable balance between the paraphrastic and literal so skillfully maintained in the official Targumim. That formed a necessary condition with the regulations of the reading in early as in later ages.

The Lxx assumed the same course. There was sought an exact rendering, a simple and ground understanding, as close to the original as possible. Literalness was insisted upon and expository rendering would only be tolerated in difficult or poetical passages, or where the danger of a misinterpretation had to be averted. I completely disagree with Zunz, Geiger, Bacher [54] and others, who insist on the priority of the Mid-rashic Targum to the literal. Their theory is wrong. It is built upon, it would seem, the doubtful foundation that the poetical and difficult passages were first to be rendered.[56] But as they can furnish no evidence it is just as safe to assert that the simpler passages involving a literal rendering were rendered either first or at one time with the poetical ones. Invoking again the Lxx, the literalness is the conspicuous feature in them and not the paraphrastic. The exposition of the Law and the Prophets held on the Sabbaths in the synagogue in Alexandria left little trace in the Lxx. Nothing approaching the Philonian exposition has

---

20). Com. Tischendorf, V. T. G. XIII; Geiger, Urschrift, 160; König, Einleitung, 103.

54) Zunz, G. V., 344; Geiger, Ur., 425. Com. Frankel, Über d. Zeit etc., Ver. Deut. Orient, 1845, 13. Bacher ib. 64, after assert-ing that the literalness of Onkelos was a later and Babylonian tendency, is not in the least disturbed when, following this assertion, he draws a list of cases in which Onkelos is expository while the Frag., the original and oldest, according to his view, is literal. Com. also Ps. Jon. Deut. 33:26 rendering the v. literally, while Onk. and Frag. are exegetical.

55) Com. Steinschneider, Jewish Lit. (Heb.) 20. He also takes the view that the Targum in essence was not different from the Midrash, assuming that the Targum originated from single translation of difficult words. Like Geiger and Bacher, he asserts (ib. 190) that from these (Midrashic) Targumim resulted the simpler and exacter understanding of the Bible. It is certainly a curious and queer process.

found room in the translation. It was the knowledge and not the exposition of the Bible which formed the prime necessity for instituting the reading of the translation. These writers have exaggerated innocent sayings in the Mishna reproaching ren-derings of certain targumists, which are found in Ps. Jonathan. Because they are cited in the Mishna and because they were re-jected, they came at once to be regarded not only as belonging to an early Targum but to the earliest. Consequently, the ex-position preceded in point of time the literal which marked a new departure and had been accomplished in Babylonia. But these citations could as well belong to a later Targum. On the contrary, the way they are quoted ואלין דמתרגמין [56] clearly signifies the existence of another Targum upon which these new Targumim had attempted to encroach. [57]

Again, it should be borne in mind that the Agada had been the product of a generation subsequent to the simple exposition of the Soferim and the Zugoth. The exegetical element in the Targumim was influenced, and on occasion determined, by the Halaka, which also had a progressive history. But the Targum existed before the new tendencies made their appearance.

The official Targumim thus represent the early as well as the later recognized Targumim used in public worship. Through common use there had been a continuous interchange of influence between them. It is customary to consider the T. to the Pentateuch as older than the T. to the Prophets. [58] This opinion rests on a questionable argument. There can be no doubt that the introduction of the Targum in public service dates back to a comparatively early period. But in my judgment it had not originated before the Maccabean age. [59] There is suf-ficient evidence in support of the view that Hebrew had not

---

56) Y. Berakoth 5, 3: ואילין דמתרגמין עמא דבני ישראל במה דאנן האומר ומזרער לא תתן :רחמן בשמיא. The other citation in Megilla 25a reads למלך which carries the same implication.

57) Com. Z. Chajoth on Megilla 25a.

58) It is interesting to note that later tradition also assigns to the Targum to Pent. an earlier date. Com. Sifri beginning וזאת הברכה. Com. Maimonidas מימות עזרה תקנו שיהא שם תורגמן לעם : חל' תפלה, יב מה שהקורא קורא בתורה ; of the T. to the Prophets he proceeds only to repeat the regulations appearing in the Mishna.

59) Com. Kautzsch Gram. d. Biblisch-Aram., p. 4.

only been well understood in Palestine in the time of Ezra and Nehemaia, but that it had been the vernacular tongue.[60] There is, on the contrary, no positive evidence either that Aramaic had been in those early days the vernacular among the Jews in Palestine or even that the general ignorance of the Jews of the Aramaic tongue of the period of the Kings had entirely passed. What use would that generation have for an Aramaic version of the Law ?

But whether it had been introduced in the period immediately preceding the Maccabean uprising or in the early days of Maccabean rule, it is certain that when the need of the Targum arose there had already been established the custom of reading in public service from the Prophets as a supplement to the reading from the Law. As the reading from the Law goes back to Ezra,[61] and because of the greater interest in the knowledge

---

60) Frankel, Paläst. Ex., 208, 280, consistent with his literal interpretation of the tradition that the Targum originated with Ezra, accepts the genial but useless theory put forward by De Rossi (l. c.) that Onkelos was consulted by the Greek translators. But unlike De Rossi, Frankel would not consider the Aramaic version—a corrupted rendering of the original. Rapaport, זכרון לאחרונים Let. 3, takes the same view, and it should be followed by all others of the same mind as regards the date of the origin of the Targum. To overlook the difficulty arising from an assumption that either the Targum had not been carried to Egypt, or, being in use, that it exercised no influence on the Lxx, would certainly be unforgiveable.

61) The Karaites ascribe the reading of the Haftora to Ezra (com. Neubauer, Aus Petersburger Bibliothek, p. 14); Abudraham placed its origin in the persecutions of Antiochus. But whatever cause one may unearth (com. Büchler J. Q. R. v., p. 6 et seq.), one outstanding cause was the institution of the reading of the Law in public service. The reading from the Prophets served the purpose of administering an admonition as to the holiness and observance of the Law. I completely agree with Büchler that the introduction of the reading of the Pentateuch had its origin in the festivals (J. Q. R., v. 5, p. 442). Thus the Sifra to Lev. 23:43; Sifri to Deut. 16:1; Meg. 4a, 32a. The Law was read by Ezra on the festivals of the New Year and Tabernacles (Neh. 8:2, 8, 18; 9:3). The reading on Saturday appears to have arisen later, when synagogues arose outside Jerusalem. Hence the supposition that the selection of definite portions for each festival preceded the definite apportioning of the Sabbatical reading. I disagree, however, with the motive to which Büchler attributes the origin of both the Pentateuchal

of the Law, the necessity of an Aramaic translation of the Law might have been earlier appreciated than that of the Prophets. But no sooner was the reading from the Prophets instituted than the necessity of an Aramaic rendering became apparent. Although the Greek translation of the Pentateuch leads all other books of the Bible in point of time, not even a century passed before the Prophets "and the other writings" were to be found in the Greek tongue.

As far as the general ordinance is concerned, no distinction is made between the Targum to the Law and the Targum to the Prophets. Accordingly, it is said in Soferim 18:4 ומן הדין לתרגם לעם ולנשים ותינוקות כל סדר ונביא של שבת לאחר קריאת התורה. In the Mishna Meg. 21a, 23b; Yerushalmi 4, 1, 5, the Targum to the Prophets is discussed alongside with the Targum to the Law, the limitations on the reading of the former being less rigid than the latter for other reasons דלא נפקא מיניה הוראה. Again in Mishna 25a; Tosefta 4 (3); Y. Meg. 4, 11 a list of passages both from the Law and the Prophets is given which were not to be translated. Both were not considered obligatory, so that their omission in the service would not call for repetition, as it is made clear in Y. Meg. 4, 6 והתרגום מעכב? אומר רב

___

and Prophetical readings, which would place their institution at nearly the same date. One should not resort to the magical Samaritan influence in order to find the cause for such an ordinance when it is readily presented in Nehemia: "And on the second day there gathered themselves together unto Ezra, the expounder, to obtain again intelligence of the words of the Law. And they found written in the Law that the children of Israel should dwell in booths during the feast in the seventh month. And (they ordered) that they should publish... throughout all their cities and through Jerusalem saying, go forth unto the mountain and fetch leaves to make booths, as it is written (13-15)." It was the ignorance of the people of the ordinances of the festivals which formed the cause of the reading from the book of the Law. These passages present sufficient ground for ascribing the ordinance of the reading from the Law to Ezra. This might also be implied in the tradition ascribing it to Moses. Com. B. Kama 82a. The Haftora is much later, and dates to the end of the third century or the beginning of the second century B. C. Direct and positive evidence cannot be furnished. Early tradition is silent over it. But what has been said above and the fact that a Greek translation of the Prophets had already been made at that time, and also the mention of the Prophets in Ben Sira in a manner suggesting general acquaintance with them by the people, lend support to this view.

יוסה מן מה דאנן חמיין רבנן נפקין לתעניתא וקדאין ולא מתרגמין הרה.
אמרה שאין התרגום מעכב . This is in substance implied in the
saying of R. Chalafta b. Saul, Meg. 24a, as interpreted in Tosafoth l. c.

But the reading from the Law and from the Prophets in
the Sabbath service had not been definitely set as late as in the
time of the composition of the Mishna. The selection was left
to the discretion of the individual community. Any portion
from the Prophets, as from the Law, would be read.[62] The
readings were translated. Hence the rise of a Targum to all the
Prophetical books. The author of the official Targumim was
the congregation. The Targum in its first stages had no definite
shape. The reader framed the translation at the reading of the
original. Every reader had his own choice of words and his
own way of rendering. He was only conditioned to present a
close and exact rendering.

But with the persistence of the Targum and its growing
significance the free translation progressed by various degrees
to a definite and unchangeable form. Anything which endures

---

62) Com. Maimonides **ונראה שלא חיה** : בסף משנה, הל' תפלה, יב, יב
להם באותו זמן הפטורות קבועות כמונג חיום אלא כל אחד חיה מפטור ענין
שנראה לו שהוא מתיחס לפרשה . The same may be applied to the reading
of the Law. Only the reading on the festivals, including the New
Moon, Purim and Chanuka, the Four Shabbaths, Maamodoth and days
of fasting, are indicated (Babli, Meg. Mish. 30b; Y. Mish. 3, 4, 5, 6, 7).
There is no hint of a definite Sabbatical reading. The words **חוזרין לכסדרן**
(Y. Meg. 3, 5, 7; Babli 29a, 31a) should not be taken literally. The
interpretation of R. Ami and Jeremia Meg. 30b refers to a time when
there was a definite reading both from the Law and P. Had there been
definite portions for the Sabbatical readings from the Law, there would
certainly be also a definite selection of parallel Prophetical readings.
There could be no reason why there should be a discrimination against
the Prophetical reading. I am fully convinced that there existed a definite
Prophetical reading for each festival enumerated in the Mishna. It is
true, that in both Y. and B. the reading from the Law is given while no
mention is made of the Prophetical readings. But the Tosefto, while
registering for the festival only the readings from the Law, is, however,
indicating for the Four Sabbaths the Prophetical readings side by side
with the reading from the Law. If there had existed definite Prophetical
readings for the Four Sabbaths, there had certainly been definite Prophetical readings for the more important festivals, and yet no mention
of them is made in the Tosefto. The reason may be simple: it mentions

in humanity, as in the universe, tends to shape. It had become necessary to lay down certain rules to regulate the translation. How is the verb or adjective of a collective noun to be rendered: in singular, as in original, or in the plural? Is the literal sense to be considered or the implied meaning? How about the anthropo-morphic expressions, shall they be rendered literally to the an-noyance of the worshippers or explained away, and how? There are passages involving a Halakic interpretation of great import-ance, or a controversial point between the parties; shall such passages be left over to the intelligence of the reader, who might not be trained in the Halaka? A way of rendering had to be early devised, which the reader was to follow. The first attempts at uniformity were directed towards single phrases or words. Gradually they spread to include the less dangerous regions. The Rabbis, by concerted authority at each time, were responsible for the change. An excellent illustration is furnished us in Y. Meg. 4, 1 and Bik. 3, 4. In one case it is the rendering of טנא (Deut. 26:2). The targumist rendered מנא, but R. Jona, holding it to be improper to present the first fruits in any other receptacle than a basket, objected to this rendering and insisted upon the rendering of סלא, as the Targumim to the Pent. have it. Another case was מצות ומרורים (Exod. 12:8), which the targumist rendered פטירין עם ירקונן; the rendering ירקונן being

the more important, the Pentateuchal reading. The same may be said of the Mishna also.

But we know that there were no definite Prophetical readings for the Sabbath. The Mishna points out certain portions from the Prophets which are not to be read. Y. Meg. 4, 11 מרכבה : דוד ואמנון Y. Meg. 4, 12; Babli 25a, while according to R. Eliezer בחודע את ירושלים (Ez. 16) should not be read.

Had the passages represented a definite Sabbatical reading, a sub-stitute reading would be indicated which should be read instead of the interdicted ones.

It should be borne in mind that all these portions from the Prophets cited in the Tosefta (ibid), with the exception of Ezek. 1, have not found a place on the calendar of the Haftora. The attempt of Büchler to discover the early divisions of the readings from the Law and the accompanied readings from the Prophets is highly hypothetical. Again, the definite mention of the Targum in the Mishna and Tosefta shows that the Targum was introduced before a definite order of the Sab-batical readings had been introduced.

misleading as to the proper kind, Jeremiah would force the targumist to retranslate it in a different way. The third case concerned the rendering of תורים ובני יונה (Lev. 5:7), and R. Pineas
would not allow to render תורים by פטימין. These cases demonstrate the peculiar manner in which the composition of the T.
was accomplished.

Although the official Targumim were in a definite shape in
the time of R. Akiba,[63] the process of transformation had been
still going on to a comparatively late date. It affected both the
literal and exegetical rendering. Some older exegetical renderings were rejected and replaced by others. Of the rejected, some
have been preserved in the Ps. Jonathan, which in itself is an
Aramaic Jalqut comprising also later Agadic material. Rejected
paraphrases of the Targum to the Prophets might be those which
appear on the margin in the Codex Reuch. and in some early
editions. Although the notes prefaced תרגום א' contain Agadic
material of a later date, they contain elements which might have
been first incorporated in the Targum but rejected later as not to
be read in the service. The same may be said of those ascribed to
ספר א' although being on the whole an attempt to simplify and
to supplement the extant T. Again, the duplicate renderings
which are found both in Jonathan and Onk. can be explained by
the fact that one formed the older explanation while the other
represents a more recent one but which for some reason had
not succeeded in dispossessing the older one. This explains also
the curious renderings of certain verses, one half retaining one
rendering while the other half contains a remnant of a different rendering. As rejected paraphrases may be considered the
Targum to Micah 7:3, quoted in Rashi, and another quoted in
the name of Jehuda of Paris on 2S 6:11.[64]

---

63) Com. R. Akiba's homily on Zek. 12:1 (Moed Katan 28a),
whcih shows that R. Akiba knew the Targum to this verse. Com. R.
Jehuda's saying referred to above; also Beraitha Baba Kama 17a
וכבוד עשו לו במותו זה חזקיה מלך יהודה שיצאו לפניו שלשים וששה אלף
חלוצי כתף. דברי ר' יהורה. א"ל נחמיה, והלא לפני אחאב עשו כן.

64) Com. Zunz, G. V. 80: מצא חרב זללה בשם יהודה מפריש מפזז
יונתן תרגם Ezek. 27:17: . ומכרכר תר' ירוש' טדויי ופיוטי. Com. also Rashi,
חטי מנית ופנג בחטי רי חוש... מפי ר' שמעון מצאתי שמצא במקרא התרגום
ירושלמי רחושלא וקלמא.

The same can be said of the selection of words in the rendering. It should be noticed at the outset that the remarkable unity exhibited in the official Targumim is strongly emphasised also in the wording of the translation. Once the Aramaic word was set for a Hebrew word, you are certain to find it in each case where this Hebrew word occurs. An illustration of this amazing fact is presented in the rendering of the names of peoples, countries and cities. Other instances can be picked up at random. It demonstrates in a most emphatic way the scrupulous rigor with which the work of the Aramaic rendering had been accomplished. If, therefore, a word is rendered in one place one way and another way somewhere else, we are certain to have two different Targumim of the word in question. But apart from cases of this sort which are contained in the official Targumim, variations have come down to us from different sources. Concerning Onkelos variations are contained in Ps. Jonathan. In some cases in which Ps. Jonathan has a different Aramaic word for the Hebrew from that contained in Onk., the Fragmentary will be found to correct it, replacing it by the one used in Onkelos. There is, however, no means enabling us to discover which of the two represents the earlier form. They might have had their origin in the same time. Two communities might have coined them at the same time. Instructive instances are presented in the different renderings given by Rav and Levi of Gen. 49:27 (Zebachim 54a); ib. 30:14 (San. 99a), Onkelos agreeing with that of the former; R. Jehuda and Nehemia—of Gen. 18:1 (Gen. r. 42, 6). Variations of this kind are not wanting also in the Targum to the Prophets. Some have been preserved in Jonathan. A good many others are contained in Talmud and Midrashim and in the marginal notes in the Codex Reuch., under the names of ת״א, ס״א, ל״א, פליג, ואית דמתרגמי. In a few cases of the latter the variant will be seen to agree with Ps. Jonathan and Fragmentary. This fact lends new support to the view of the common source of all Targumim. The former cases shall be considered first.

מישר—ל״א . So is בעלת...Targum בעלת באר Joshua 19:8 the T. of בעל גד (ib. 11:17; 12:7) בעל חרמ׳ (Jud. 3:3) בעלת תמר (Jud. 20:33) etc.

בספל אדירים ; λεκάνη Targum לקנא הספל Judges 6:38

(ib. 5:25) Targum בפילי גבריא. The latter is the rendering of קבעת (Is. 51:17, 22). So is rendered קערת כסף (Num. 7:13) in Ps. Jon.; Onk. מגסתא.

Judges 8:21 השהרנים Targum ענקיא; in Is. 3:18 it is rendered by סבכיא. The latter is given to Judges by ל"א in Cod. Reuch.

1S. 19:13, 16; Ez. 21:26; Za. 10:2 תרפים Targum צלמניא. Judges 18:17, 18, 20 דמאין while ל"א has עביטא.

ib. 16 וכביר העזים Targum ונדא דעיזיא. But ל"א has וגונכא. This is the rendering of במכבר (2K 8:15) connected with כביר. Com. Kimchi l. c.

1K 22:49 תרשיש Targum אפריקא. So Jer. 10:9; Jonah 1:3. But Is. 2:16; 23:1, 14; Ezek. 27:12 ימא.

2K 5:23 חרטים Targum פלדסים. Is. 3:22 מחכיא.

Jerem. 31:28 כאשר שקדתי עליהם Targum כמו דחשבת; in the second half כן אשקד Targum כן יחדי מימרי. The same was certainly the rendering of כאשר שקדתי which is found in ס"א. Here is a case of a rejected Anthropomorphism of a latter time.

Ezek. 27:6 כתים Targum אפוליא or איטליא. Everywhere else it is rendered כתאי (Is. 23:1 etc.).

Ezek. 27: 21 קדר Targum נכט. Otherwise ערבאי(Is. 21:16, 17; 42:11; 60:7. So T. to Ps. 120:5.).

Ezek. 27:23 ערן Targum חדיב. This is the rendering of אשכנז (Jerem. 51:27).

Ezek. 40:19 התחתונה Targum מציעאה; איתדמי — ארעאה. So is the rendering of התחתונה in v. 18.

Ezek. 45:2; 48:17 ומגרשיהם—ורוחיהון. Ib. 27:28 T. פרויא As Ps. Jon. and F. Lev. 25:34. On. וחקל רוח.

Am. 2:7; Is. 47:6 לחלל Targum לאפסא. So Ps. Jon. Exod. 20:25. Is. 48:41; Ezek. 20:39 Targum תחלון. But אית דמתרגמי לאחלא Am. l. c.

Com. further Kimchi Ezek. 40:16.

To these cases may be added the following cases, which Cod. Reuch. is at variance with the extant Targum, the latter being supported by ל"א.

Jerem. 17:7 מבטחו Targum בסעריה; ל"א — רוחצניה. So in extant T.

Ez. 9:10 דרכם Targum חוביהין; ל"א — אורחיהין; in the extant T. פורענות אורחיהון.

Micah 3:11 מסתמכין‎ .So in ‏מסתמכין — ל"א ; רחיצין‎ Targum ‏ייעני‎
the extant T.

Cases in which the marginal variations follow the Ps. Jon.:
Jud. 8:11 ‏פלנישו‎ Targum ‏ולהונתיה ; ל"א — ופילקתיה‎. So Ps.
Jon. Gen. 22:24, Onk. agreeing with Jon.

1K 4:6 ‏הבית‎ Targum ‏ביתא ; ל"א — קורטור‎. So Ps. Jon.
Num. 22:18; 24:13. On. follows Jon.

Other cases of variants:
1. ‏עיפושין — '5"א ; כיסנין‎ Targum ‏נקודים‎ Joshua 9:5.
2. ‏גשריא — ל"א ; מחצביא‎ Targum ‏פסילים‎ Jud. 3:19.
3. ‏ישרל — ל"א ; ופיים‎ Targum ‏וישמע‎ 1S 24:8.
4. ‏פרסין — ל"א ; רטישין‎ Targum ‏נטשים‎ 1S 30:16.
5. ‏לונכיין—ל"א ; γαισονὶ ; גיססין‎ Targum ‏שבטים‎ 2S 18:14.
6. ‏אספקלריא — ל"א; מחזיתא‎ Targum ‏הגליונים‎ IS. 3:23.
the Greek σπεχλάριον Lat. specularia. Here is presented a case,
where seemingly a Greek word was replaced by its Aramaic
equivalent. The same was the case with Onkelos. Bacher (ib.)
has made this point clear by a comparison between Onk. and
Ps. Jon. and the Frag. That is true to some extent also of Jon.,
which is demonstrated in the Greek and its Aramaic substitute of
‏ומגרשיהם‎ cited above. Still, Jonathan appears to have been more
immune to such an attempt than even Ps. Jonathan. Here is
an instructive case: ‏שקל‎ (Ez. 4:10) is rendered by the Greek
‏פילם‎ φόλλις while all—Onk., Ps. Jon. and Frag.—render it by
‏סלע‎ (Num. 7:13 etc.).
7. ‏מצית — ס"א ; אעדית‎ Targum ‏מצית‎ IS. 51:17.
8. ‏כסמא — ס"א ; ספרא יספרון‎ Targum ‏כסום יכסמון‎ Ez. 44:20
‏יכסמון‎.

Two cases, one in ‏ס"א‎, the other in ‏ל"א‎, vary with Jon.
in anthropomorphisms: ‏למימרי—ס"א ; לותי‎ .T (Jerem. 31:38) ‏אלי‎;
‏לפולחני — ל"א ; יתי‎ .T (ib. 16:11) ‏אותי‎. These cases and the
case of Jerem. 31:27 cited above reinforce the view set forth
above that later usage eliminated some anthropomorphic substitutes from the T.

The following are cases of variations found in the Talmud
and Midrash.
Joshua 16:8 ‏תאנת שלה‎ Targum ‏תאנת שלה‎. Y. Meg. 1, 12
‏איסכופיה דשילה‎.

Y. San. 2, 4 . כדין לחייך Targum ואמרתם בה לחי IS. 25:6
לקיימא. So Onk. and Ps. Jon. Deut. 4:4.

Y. Taanith 4, 5 . מטול כם דלוט Targum מישא בערב IS. 21:13
מטול רב בערב .

IS. 21:5 סדרו פתורין אקימו Targum ערך השלחן צפה הצפית
and in Cant. r. סדר פתורא סדר מנרתא 9 ,63 .Gen. r . סוכתא
סדרת פתורא, אקימת מנרתא, אדלקת בוצינא. מישחו, כמעט שעברתי
מגן — קבלו מלבותא. They agree with Jon. only in the rendering of
ערך השלחן.The citation from Cant. r. contains two recensions.
The rendering אדלקת בוצינא agrees with Cod. Reuch. and is
identical with the marginal note headed תרג' ירוש .

— כי עלית כלך לגנות Psichta Lamentation r. on Is. 22:1, 2
ולאיגדא סלקין להון ; עיר הומיה — קרתא מערבבתא ; קריה עליזה —
קריה חדתא; מהומה ומבוסה ומבוכה — יום מעורבב, יום רביזה,
יום דבכיא.
קרתא מישבחתא, כרבא חדאה, ארי יום רגיט ואתדשא וקטול. .But T
ויגל מסך יהודה — גליא דכבא Targum וגליית ib. IS. 22:8
מטמורת .

ib. on Ez. 24:6 אוי עיר הדמים סיר אישר חלאתה בה —
אוי מן קמא דקרתא דישפכו דמים בגווה, וחפשושיתה לא נפקת מן גווה ;
דחפשישיתה בגווה — וחלאתה לא יצאת ממנה Targum וי על קרתא
דאישדי דם זכאי. דהיא כדורא דזיהומתיה ביה וזיהומתיה לא נפקת מניה.

שבחות דהיכלא ; — והילילו שדות היכל Cant. r. 1:1 on Am. 8:3
חלף זמרא . Targum

אריא אריא גברא—הוי אריאל אריאל Y. Shabbath 6, 4 on IS. 29:1
מדבחא, מדבחא . Targum

קלופי סובלתא — חישפי שובל on IS. 47:2 כמעט שעברתי .Cant. r
אתהברי שלטוניך Targum ; דנהרא .

Koheleth r. ואת האומנות on 2K 18:16 טובה חכמה מה היא —
סקופיא. Targum האומנות ? בי לוי אמר ציפריא ורבנן אמרין שיגריא.

Lev. r. 4:1 on Is. 1:21 ועתה מרצחים — עבידין קטוליא . Jon.
קטולי נפש . Shochar Tob 32, 2 (com. Y. San. 10, 1) on Mi. 7:8
ומעבר על חובין Jon. . דאינשי חובין — על פשע .

Similar cases are: Lev. r. 5, 2; Num. r. 10, 5 on Am. 6:4
and Lev. r. 6, 2 on Zech. 5:1, all of which represent, undoubtedly,
a different and rejected Targumic rendering. The following case
is to my mind an interesting relic of a rejected rendering. This

is in Frag. Deut. 32:1: דכן הוא מפריש ואמר טולו לישמיא עיניכון
ואסתכלו לארעא מלרע ארי שמיא כתננא ימסין וארעא כלבושא תבלי.
The rendering in Jon. is as follows: זקיפו לישמיא עיניכון ואסתכלו
בארעא מלרע ארי שמיא כתננא דערי בן יערו וארעא ככסותא דבליא
כן תבלי The rendering in the F. is literal. We cannot determine
which is the earlier rendering.

The process of alteration had been going on until a comparatively late date but not so late as the final redaction of the
Babylonian Talmud. That was made especially possible by the
fact that the T. was recited in the worship by heart. Reading
the Targum from a written copy was prohibited. This interdiction is indicated in Tanchuma Gen. 18:17:

ילמדנו רבינו מי שהוא מתרגם לקורא בתורה מה היא שיסתכל בכתב ?
כך שנו רבותינו המתרגם אסור להסתכל בכתב. אמר ר' יהודה בן פזי
מקרא מלא הוא : כתב לך את הדברים האלה — הרי המקרא ; כי על
פי הדברים האלה — הרי התרגום שניתן בעל פה.

This passage is quoted in the Pesiqta (ed. Friedmann), p.
28. Does it imply an interdiction to put the Targum into writing?

This question was the cause of much contention. Rashi
inclined to an extreme interpretation of the prohibition to write
down all belonging to traditional exposition. So with regard
to the Mishna which, he insists, was not written down
by Rabi (Ketuboth 19b). Com. Rashi Erubin 62a, beginning
והכי נקט מגילת תענית שלא היתה דבר הלכה כתובה בימיהם : כגון
אפילו אות אחת חוין ממגלת תענית; also Taanith 12a. He takes
the view that the Targum had not been allowed to be written
down. Commenting on the Mishna Shabbath 115a he says:
ורבותי פרשו דהאי בכל לשון דקאמר אבתובין קאי ולא אנביאין, דעפ"י
שכתובין בכל לשון טעונין גניזה, ומדומה אני מפני שמצינו ביונתן בן
עוזיאל שאמרו תרגום הן מפרשין כך, ואני אומר אף בנביאים, אם אמר
יונתן לא כתבו ולא נתנו להכתב, והכי מפרש במס' מגלה דמאן דאסר
בכולהו אסר.

According to Rashi's teachers, with whom he disagrees, not
only was the T. to the Prophets written down, but also allowed
to be read in the service in written form; for, as Rashi himself remarks, one is dependent upon the other. For this reason
it was seemingly his teachers who would interpret the contention
between Rab Huna and Rab Chisda as referring only to the

Hagiographa, as according to the interpretation of the Gemarah they only differ on the view of those who prohibit the reading from a written Targum. Rashi, however, makes capital of the expression in the Babli Meg. 3a אונק׳ הגר אמרו as does Luzzatto (O. G. IX). But as the saying of R. Jeremia is also quoted in the Yerushalmi, it is just as well to take אמרו as an innocent substitute for תרגם of the Yerushalmi version, which does not carry this implication. The main source of Rashi's contention is the prohibition contained in the saying of Rabban Simon b. Gamliel, Y. M. 1, 9; Babli 8b אף בכפרים לא התירו שיכתבו אלא יונית. But there are the חכמים (ib. and Shab. 115b) who differ with him, and as it is said in Soferim 15,2 אף על פי שאמר רבן שמעון בן גמליאל שאף בכפרים לא התירו לכתב אלא יונית, לא הורו לו חכמים שאמרו מעשה ברשב״ג (רבן גמליאל) שהיה עומד... ואף חכמים עמדו בדבריהם שאמרו כל כתבי הקודש ואף על פי שכתובין בכל ל׳שון טעונים גניזה.

Furthermore, there is no implication in R. Simon b. Gamliel's saying of a prohibtion to write down the T. He only meant to say that the reading from a written T. in service does not fulfil the required Aramaic rendering. Consequently, as Rab Porath, quoted in Tosafoth (Shab. ib. ולא) rightly put it, because it is not allowed to read it, is equivalent to reading the Torah by heart and דברים שבכתב אי אתה רשאי לאמרם בעלפה. The question raised there against it is thus well answered. Com. also Tos. Sota 33a כב. There is certainly not the slightest ground for an inference that no written T. to the Prophets existed. Witness the interpretation (in Babli ib.) of R. Jehuda ורבותינו התירו יונית אמר ר׳ יהודה אף כשהתירו אבותינו לא התירו אלא בספר תורה. But we well know that at that time all the books of the Bible existed in the Greek translation. There is the same baselessness for the reason ascribed by Luzzatto (l. c.), Zunz (G. V. 65) and others to the prohibition, namely, that the T. containing some Halaka, was regarded on one plane with תורה שבע״פ which was not to be written down (Temura 14b, Gittin 60b). Had this been the reason, how was the Lxx sanctioned by all the Rabbis, containing as it does so many Halakic interpretations? (Com. Z. Frankel דרכי המישנה 10 and Über d. Einfluss l. c.). It should also be noticed that the reason given for R. Simon b. Gamliel's interdiction of other than the Greek translation is

שאין התורה יכולה לתרגם כל צרכה and not because it belongs to the
דברים שבע"פ .

On the other hand, it is well known that in spite of the
interdiction on the written Halaka, the Rabbis did not hesitate
to write down for private use Halakic decisions and intercourses.
It will also be remembered that in the time of Rabban Gamliel
the Elder there was already in existence a Targum to Job. That
the interdiction passed by him on this Targum was not
due to the fact of its being written was shown above. Again,
Esther had also been translated, as it appears from the Mishna
Meg. 17a: הקורא את המגלה קרא תרגום בכל לישון לא יצא...לא צריכה
דכתיב תרגום וקרי תרגום . The reason is pointed out, for it
is written ככתבם וכלשונם . But there could be no more reason
for considering the T. to the Prophets דברים שבע"פ than the T.
to Esther.

It is clear then that the prohibition against the written T.
had only been instituted against the public reading in the service.
The reason for that was mainly to avert sharing by the T. the
same sanctity with the original. This is in essence the very
reason given for R. Simon b. Gamliel's view. And this prohibition, it would seem, was enforced even at a date when the
Mishna was already written down and allowances were made
for the written Agada (com. Gittin 60b). Rapoport (זכרון
letter 3) well expounded the case of the written Halaka when he
said that the prohibition was directed mainly against the public
discussion and was not intended to exclude it from private use.
Berliner (On. 89) rightly applied this view to the T. This view
might be substantiated by Tanchuma (ib.) ואסור למתרגם ברבים
להסתכל בתורה , which Friedmann (Pesiqta ib.) is inclined to emend
להסתכל בכתב . The implied indication is that a written T.
may be permitted for private use.

There certainly were in existence written copies of the
Targum, which were restricted to personal use. One such copy
a targumist would employ in public worship and was hindered
by R. Samuel b. Isaac telling him, דברים שנאמרו בפה — בפה,
ודברים שנאמרו בכתב — בכתב (Y. Meg. 4, 5). What he meant
amounted to saying that the T. should be read by heart, just
as the original is to be read from the written only.

Targum Jonathan was used by later targumists. It was
pointed out above that Targum Ps. 18 is a copy with minor
modifications, notice of which will be taken in the chapter on
Other Targumim, of the Targum to Samuel 22. T. Jonathan
was used by the targumist of Chronicles.

The T. to Chronicles exhibits pronounced and independent
characteristics. It pursues, on the whole, its own way of exposition and translation. It is more Midrashic than the official
Targumim. He will not, in most cases, let himself be influenced
by the official Targumim. In some instances he will neither follow Onkelos nor Ps. Jonathan. Yet, even this targumist made
definite and considerable use of the Targum Jonathan. The cases
in question are of a typical nature, which do not admit of an
incidental agreement. I will quote them in order of Chronicles.

1 Chronicles 11:11 עצמך ובשרך Targum קריבך ובסרך . Jon.
2S 5:1.

1 Ch. 13:7 וירכיבו את ארון Targum ואחיתו . Jon. 2S 6:3.

1 Ch. 13:9 גרן כידון Targum אתר מתקן . Jon. 2S 6:6.

ib. שמטו Targum מרגוהו . Jon. ib.

1 Ch. 14:1 וחרשי קיר Targum ואומנין לבנין כותלא ואדריכלין דאומנין . Jon. 2S 5:11.

1 Ch. 14:9 ויפשטו בעמק רפאים Targum ויתרטישו במישר גיבוריא . Jon. 2S 5:18 reading וינטשו .

1 Ch. 14:11 בעל פרצים Targum מישר פרצים . Jon. 2S 5:20.

ib. 2S. כפרץ מים Targum דמלי מיין כתבור מאן דפחר . Jon. ib.

1 Ch. 14:15 כי יצא האלהים לפניך להכות Targum ארום נפק . Jon.2S 5:24. מלאכה מן קדם יי לאצלחא קדמך למקטל.

1 Ch. 16:3 אשפר Targum פלוג . Jon. 2S 6:19.

1 Ch. 17:1 בבית ארזים Targum בכיורי ארזיא . Jon.
2S 7:2, 7. דמטלל.

ib. וארון... תחת יריעות Targum וארונא שרי במשכנא בגוי . יריעתא . Jon. 2S 7:2.

1 Ch. 17:7 אני לקחתיך מן אחרי הצאן להיות נגיד Targum . אנא דברתיך מן דירא מבתר ענא למהוי מלכא . Jon. 2S 7:8. The
usual rendering of נגיד in the T. to Chronicles is ארכון
(1 Ch. 11:2) פרכון (1 Ch. 13:1).

Jon. 2S 7:10. אתר מתקן Targum ושמתי מקום 1 Ch. 17:9

Jon. . לית אנא במיסת Targum מי אני יי אלהים 1 Ch. 17:16
2S 7:18.

Jon. 2S 7:19. לעלמא דאתי Targum ותדבר למרחוק 1 Ch. 17:17

בכל די שמענא Targum בכל אשר שמענו באזנינו 1 Ch. 17:20
ואמרו קדמנא . Jon. 2S 7:22.

עמא יחידאי ובחיר בארעא Targum גוי אחד בארץ 1 Ch. 17:21
עמא חד בחיר... Jon. 2S 7:23

Jon. 2S . מלכו אקים לך Targum לבנות לו בית 1 Ch. 17:25
7:27.

Jon. 2S 8:2, 6. . נטלי פרס Targum נשאי מנחה 1 Ch. 18:2

Jon. 2S 8:3 . לאשנאה תחומיה Targum להציב ידו 1 Ch. 18:3
להשיב ידו .

Jon. 2S 12:13 . ומסר יתהון Targum ויׂשר במגרה 1 Ch. 20:3
וישם...

ואשרינון בקרוי Targum ויניחם בערי הרכב ועם המלך 2 Ch. 1:14
רתיכיא בר מן מה דהוו עם... . So Jon. 1K 10:26.

2 Ch. 2:9 . חטין פרנום Targum חטים מכות 1K 5:25
חטים מכלת .

TEXTUAL VARIATIONS IN JONATHAN

Jonathan, like Onkelos, deviates in many cases from the Masoretic reading to which allusion was already made in the previous chapter. There is a way to differentiate the paraphrastic from the literal sense. Out of the obscurity of the exegetical expansion there comes forth the simple, written phrase on which it rests. The Targum Jonathan, although, on the whole, far from literal adhesion to the text, is unmistakably careful to transmit both the sense and version of the text. The literal predominates in the historical portions of the Prophets. Any rendering ,then, not in accord with the Masoretic reading constitutes a deviation from the reading.

This fact was noticed by the rabbinical authorities. Rashi, while for the most part overlooking them and even following them in evident belief that they were merely of an exegetical nature, could not escape the impression that Jonathan had a different reading. Kimchi and Minchat Shai did not hesitate to point out in the plainest language some of these deviations. They have engaged the attention of later rabbinical writers as well as the modern biblical student.[1]

On close examination the deviations will be found to con-

---

1) However, Abrahm Ibn Ezra, critic as he was, would not accept such a possibility. Thus he remarks in Safa Berura (9, 11, ed. Lippmann): ודרך אחרת ליונתן בן עוזיאל, וכלנו יודעים, כי לא היה חכם אחר ר' יוחנן בן זכאי כמוהו, ולא הגיע מעלתו להיותו כחבירו יונתן. והוא היה גדול מכולם, וראינו במקומות רבים שתפש דרך דרש להוסיף טעם, כמו אלוה מתימן יבוא (חבקוק ג, ג), כי אין ספק שהוא במו אלוה תימן... רק הוסיף טעם לפרש תימן מגזירת ימין כי התיו נוסף... וככה ביער בערב רק בעבור שאמר הכתוב ערב ולא קדר ומהשם דרש בו שהוא במו הערב. ועוד שמצא עזר במלת תלינו. והנה טעמו בערב תלינו עם הערבים... וכמוהו (ישעיה כא, יג), גם הוא ידע כי חוא במו כל מלכי הערב (מלכים א', טו), ונסתם גיא הרי (זכריה יד, ה) דרש בו משרש סתום את הדברים (דניאל יב, ר) ודרש בכה בעבור שלא אמר הנביא וברחתם (יב, ר). It is an unsuccessful attempt on his part to explain away renderings that represent a different reading.

52

sist of three distinct categories. Some of them represent an unquestionably different reading. With minor exceptions, they do
not admit of being explained away. The preponderate number
of these deviations consists of a difference in the pointing. Dif-
ferences of this kind are found in great numbers in MSS. claim-
ing the Masoretic sanction. They emanate from a period when
doubts still existed, as to the reading of certain words. Even
the scrupulously literal Aquila version contains variations from
the text. The Talmud presents abundant testimony to them.[2]
On the other hand, many of these deviations are either followed
by the Lxx and P. or they appear in them in a different form. Deviations of this description are here classed under heading "A".
There is another class of deviations of a mere grammatical character. There is a noticeable tendency on the part of the translator
to eliminate the more striking discrepancies either in the number
or in the person of the substantive in the sentence. So the tran-
lator renders them in either one or the other way. Sometimes he
subordinates all the forms of the sentences to the last in order.[4]
In some cases the reverse is true [5] and in some instances all
follow the one in the middle.[6] This principle is observed by
the Lxx and P. to some extent. But it does not appear to have
been consistently followed by the targumist. The number of exceptions by far exceeds the number of the cases where this
principle is enforced. Thus it is impossible to determine the
basic rule of this principle. It takes the appearance
of an arbitrary and haphazard device. At any rate, this group
of variations does not involve a dfferent reading. They appear
under heading "B".

There is another body of deviations which are very instructive for the biblical student. The targumist made it a rule to
render sentences which resemble one another, but differ in some

---

2) אמר לי ר' יהושע, ישמעאל אחי האיך אתה קורא כי טובים דודיך
או דודיך? א"ל דודיך : א"ל אין הדבר כן שתרי חברו מלמד עליו, לדיח
בתורתו של Mish. Aboda Zara 29b. Com. also Gen. ı. 94, 4: שמניך
ר' מאיר מצאו כתוב ובן דן חושים.

3) Com. More Nebuchim 3, 43.

4) Jerem. 9:5; 11:12.

5) Ezek. 11:19

6) Is. 26:8.

particulars occuring in different parts, in one and the same way.
A similar process had been pursued by the Rabbis.
It is the היקש and the גזירה שוה of Hillel and R. Ishmael b.Jose,[7]
which forms the seventh Mida [8] of the 32 Midoth enunciated by R. Eliezer. But while in the Halaka and Agada the con-
formation is sought mainly in the circumstances or in the legal
conditions of the cases involved, the targumist is interested in
the wording. The Samaritan text, as it is well known, will often
change a phrase to agree with a similar phrase somewhere else.[9]
The Lxx in some instances and the P. to a larger extent follow
the same rule. (Com. Frankel, Pal. Ex., p. 166.). There can
be little doubt that the author had been actuated by reflection. Rendering a phrase, the recollection of the other similar
phrase flashed through the mind of the translator to leave its
stamp upon his rendering. Mental activity of this sort accounts
for many misquotations from the Bible found in the Talmud.[10]
But this practice could not have originated from a mere un-
conscious play of recollection. The translator must have been
moved by something which he considered an imperative necessity. It will be observed that in most instances treated this
way the author was concerned in eliminating an outstanding di-
vergence in the version of the narrative of one and the same
fact.[11] Whether or not the translator pursued a definite rule
in applying this principle is difficult to determine. For the most
part the author is seen to make the passage second in order to
conform the one preceding it.

This kind of variation is placed under heading C. They
are of an interpretative nature. They do not point to a different
reading, as they were taken by many biblical students. I have

---

7) Tos. San. 7, Pirkei Aboth of R. Nathan 35, and introduction
of Sifra.

8) Com. Reifm⸗ ı, Meshib Dabor (Wien, 1866).

9) Com. Kircheim כרמי שמרון p. 37 et seq.

10) Com. Aboda Zara 24b, citing IS 15:15   אשר חמל העם
על מיטב הצאן והבקר והמשנים והכרים : מיטב הצאן והבקר אשר חמל העם
ועל כל הצאן according to v. 9, and San. 49a, citing 2S 3:27 ויכהו שם
אל החמש — החמש according to 20:10.

11) Com. Judges 7:7 and 20; 1S 4:21 and 19; 2S 12:21 and 22;
1K 13:9 and 17; 2K 9:19 and 18.

omitted all deviations of a doubtful character or consisting of an unrendered or added Waw or change of the preposition, which might be due to the distraction of a copyist or the Aramaic idiom.

GROUP A

	M. T.	Targ.	R.
Joshua 2:7	על .המעברות	עד	עד (1
" 7:5	עד ה_שברים	עד דתברונון	עד השברם (2
" 9:4	ויעשו גם הם בערמה וילכו ויצטידרו	ועבדו אף אינון בחוכמא ואזדורו וילכו	Vac. וילכו
" 11:17; 12:7	מן ההר החלק	מן טורא פליגא	חלק (3
" 13:16	על מידבא	עד מידבא	עד (4
Judges 3:2	לא ידעום	לא הוו ידעין	ידעו (5
" 9:9	דמניה מיקרין... החדלתי את דשני		
	אשר בי	ובה מתפנקין	בן (6
" 11:34	אין לו ממנו	מינה	ממנה (7
" 14:15	הלמסכנותא קריתון הלירשנו קראתם לנו		

1) So in many MSS. of Kenn. and De Rossi. Com. Kimchi. But Onk. Gen. 49:13 has it literally.

2) So P. and in marg. Syro-Hex. Com. Field Hex. and also Arab. Kimchi's explanation lacks force. Dillmann's contention (Handbuch), "dass blosse Vervolgen passt zu dieser Wirkung nicht", missed the order of the narrative—as did Herrheimer's objection that "der Verlust von 36 Mann ist keine Zertrümerung". The same could be said with much greater force of Joshua's overpowering fright (vv. 6-9). But the current interpretation that the defeat at the descent is identical with the loss of the 36 in killed told in the beginning of the v., is not at all impressive. It is rather to be assumed, which the reading of the T. unquestionably implies, that the loss of the 36 gave cause to the ensuing defeat at the descent, where the loss, it would appear, was sufficient to cause anxiety. I am inclined to believe that the reading of the T. was השברום . Com. כלי יקר . The form in itself wouldn't appear strange to the targumist, as cases of this nature are numerous.

3) So P. A. Com. Field Hex., 1. c.

4) So Sebirin. Many MSS. of Kenn. and De Rossi and extant editions follow the reading of the T.

5) So P. Lxx read ידעה

6) Probably influenced by v. 13.

7) Felt by Kimchi. So Sebirin.

	M. T.	Targ.	R.
	הלא	יתנא הלבא	הלם (1
" 19:9	לינו נא הנה חנות היום	ביתו בען הכא לחוד יומא דין	הנה (2
" 20:34	מנגד לגבעה	מדרום לגבעתא	מנגב 3
" 21:10	נגדע היום שבט אחד	איתמנע	נגרע 4
1S 2:31	וגדעתי את זרועך	תקוף זרעך	זרעך (5
" 3:2	ויהי ביום ההיא	והוא ביומיא האינון	ויהי בימים ההם (6
" 6:3	אם משלחים את ארן;	אם אתון משלחים	אם משלחים אתם (7
" 12:21	ולא תסורו כי אחרי התהו	ולא תסטון מבתר פולחניה ולא תפלחון לטעותא דאינו למא	כי Vac. (8
" 15:32	אכן סר מר המות	בבעו רבונא מריר מותא	שר (9
" 22:14	וסר אל משמעתך	ורב על משמעתך	שר (10
2S. 1:21	בלי משיח בשמן	דמשיח כדבמשיחא	בלי Vac. (1

1) Com. Kimchi. Lxx הלא vacaut. In one of the MSS. of De Rossi the Keri is הלם and Ketib הלא and in two others הלם is the Ketib. Ginsburg: לסוראי הלם כתיב הלא קרי, לנהרדעי הלא כתיב הלם קרי.

2) So Lxx Lag., otherwise לין פה חנות היום are vacant. P. לערוב הנה חנות היום vacant. The T. does not render חנות.

3) Minchat Shai: בשתי מקראות ישנות כתוב מנגב. So in many MSS. of Kenn. and De Rossi.

4) Com. Onk. Exod. 21:10. This reading is found in many MSS. of Kenn. and De Rossi.

5) The second את זרוע בית אביך is rendered תקוף דרע. If the targumist followed here the Masoretic reading there is hardly any reason why it occured to him a different reading in את זרע. Lxx read in both זרע while P. follows in both the Mesoretic reading.

6) So P. Probably influenced by v. 1.

7) So Lxx, P. and many MSS. of Kenn. and De Rossi.

8) So Lxx and P. Com. end of verse כי תהו המה Targum ארי למא אינון.

9) So P. Lxx כר vacant.

10) So Lxx. Com. P.

1) So P. and Arab. The suggestion that T. read בלי, as in Kenn. MSS. 30, is hardly tenable. It would seem that the T. considered this phrase to refer to מדם חללים. Com. Ehrlich Randglossen

	M. T.	Targ.	R.
" 5:12	וכי נשא ממלכתו	ארי מנטלא מלכותיה	נשא-נשאה (2
" 14:14	אשר לא יאספון	דלא אפשר להון ריתוספון	יאספון (3
" 15:23	על פני דרך את המדבר	על אפי אורח מדברא	את Vac. (4
" 22:44	תשמדני לראש גוים	תמניני	תשימני (5
" 23:13	שלישה מהשלשים	מגברי ריש משריתא	שלשים (6
1K. 1:18	ועתה אדני המלך	ואת...	ואתה (7
" 1:20	ואתה אדני המלך	וכען	ועתה
" 6:31	האיל מזוזות חמשית	מטקסין	החמשות (8
1K. 7:3	וכפן בארז	וחפא נכרין	וספן (9
" 8:26	יאמן נא דברך	יתקיימון כען פתגמיא	הדבר
" 8:30	ואתה תשמע אל מקום שבתך אל השמים	מאתר בית שכנתך מן שמיא	ממקום... מן השמים (10
" 8:31	ובא אלה	וייתי ויומיניה	ובא ואלה (11
" 13:6	והתפלל בעדי	ובעי מן קדמוהי	אלין (12

and Thenius Sarn., to which the expression כדבמשחא points. On the other hand, it is possible that the T. took בלי to mean annointing, from root בלל PS. 92:11. Ehrlich's assumption (ibid) that the T. read instead of תרומות שדי — לא די is founded on a misunderstanding of the T.

2) So P. Probably influenced by 1 CH. 14:2.

3) Exod. 5:7. But Com. T. to PS. 104:22.

4) So Lxx. P.
את is omitted in many MSS.

5) This is the reading in PS. 18:44. As the T. to PS. renders this word in accordance with the reading here, it is obvious that he intended to correct the rendering of Jonathan. The rendering of the T. is supported by P. and Lxx Lag.

6) Com. T. to vv. 23, 24 and Rashi and Kimchi. Onk. Exod. 14:7 felt by Kimchi. Com. Field Hex. Note 26. So Lag. Lxx.

7) So Lxx, P. and 250 MSS. Kimchi: רבים מהסופרים טעו בזאת המלה וכתבו ועתה באלף לפי שהוא קרוב לענין, אבל ברור הוא אצלנו כי הוא ועתה בעיין מפי ספרים המדויקים ומפי המסורת זהו ואתה באלף וטועים בו בעיין לפי שהענין יותר קרוב.

8) But com. T. to v. 33; 7:5. Felt by Kimchi:
וי"ת מטקסין כמו חמושים.

9) So Lxx P.

10) So P., in accordance with 2 Chronicles 6:21.

11) So Lxx P.

12) Lxx omit the whole phrase.

	M. T.	Targ.	R.
`` 13:12	ויראו בניו את הדרך	ואחזיאו	ויראו 1)
`` 16:9	בית ארצא אשר על הבית	רי בביתא	בבית 2)
`` 16:24	ויקן את ההר שומרון	וזבן ית כרכא	העיר 3) ויחלטיה
`` 20:33	ויחלטו הממנו	וחטפוהא מניה	ממנו 4)
`` 21:8	אשר בעירו	דבקרתא	בעיר 5)
`` 21:13	ויעדהו	ואסהידו	ויעדו 6)
`` 22:30	התחפש ובא	אנא אשתני ואיעול	אתחפש ואבא 7)
2K. 2:14	איה י' אלהי אליהו	קביל בעותי...	אהה 8)
`` 3:25	עד השאיר אבניה בקיר חרשת	עד דלא אשתארת אבנא בקרתא דלא פגרוה	עד השאיר בקיר הרסת 9)
`` 17:11	ויעשו דברים רעים	ועבדו קדמוהי	בעיניו 10)
`` 17:13	בידי כל נביאי כל חזה	ביד כל ספר	נביא 11)

---

1) So Lxx P. Kimchi: ת"י ואחזיאו כמו ויראו בפתח היוד מבנין הפעיל.

2) Com. Lxx. P.

3) So he renders ויבן את ההר (ib), but אדני ההר שמרן is rendered literally. It might, however, be interpretative suggested by the text, for the city—not the mountain—was called by this name. Why should the T. to Am. 3:9 render הרי שמרן literally while שומרון הר — כרכא (Am. 4:1; 6:1), although we find ערי שומרון (1K 13:32) as well, would admit of no such explanation. Cases, however, of this sort are found in the T. Kimchi (followed by Gersonide) infers from the T. that there really was a city there and Omri just strengthened it.

4) So P.; according to the Maarabai this reading is the Keri while the Masoretic reading is the Ketib.

5) Com. P. Lxx omit אשר בעירו.

6) So P.

7) So Lxx P. Felt by Kimchi. Probably interpretative suggested by what follows in the verse.

8) Or אנה (Com. 2K 20:3). Probably for anthropomorphic reasons.

9) So Lxx P. Having read הרסת and taking it to refer to אבניה the targumist changed the number.

10) Probably interpretative.

11) P. has both in plural, so that the T. might have been influenced by כל חזה.

	M. T.	Targ.	R.
`"` 21:8	ולא אוסיף להניר רגל ישראל	ולא אוסיף לטלטל ית ישראל	Vac. רגל
`"` 23:13	להר המשחית	לטור זיתיא	להר המשחה [1]
IS. 3:12	ונשים משלו בו	וכמרי חובא	נשים [2]
`"` 5:13	וכבדו מתי רעב	ויקירהון מיתו בכפנא	מתי [3]
`"` 8:14	והיה למקדש ולאבן נגף	ויהי מימריה בכון לפורען	למקדשו
`"` 8:21	וקלל במלכו ובאלהיו	ויבזי שום פתכריה וטעותיה	מלכו [4]
`"` 10:15	בהניף שבט את מרימיי כהרים מטה לא עץ	כארמא חוטרא למימחי לא חוטרא מחי אלהין מן דמחי ביה	כהניף שבט את מרימיו [5] Vac.
`"` 10:34	ונקף סבכי היער בברזל	ויקטיל גברי משריתיה דמתגברין כברזלא	כברזל
`"` 11:16	והחרים ה'...	ויבש	החריב
`"` 17:2	עזבות ערי ערער	שביקין קרויהון חרבו	ערי ערער
`"` 21:13	ביער בערב תלינו	בחורשא ברמשא	בערב [6]
`"` 23:3	ובמים רבים זרע שחר	רהות מספקא סחורא	סחר [7]

---

1) Com. Rashi and Kimchi. It is so quoted by the R. Josi, Shab. 56b. This reading is found in one MS. Kenn.

2) Felt by Rashi, Kimchi. So Lxx. A. Com. Esther r. 2, 2: ונשים משלו בו א"ר חוניא קופצין עליהן בבעל חוב.

3) So Lxx P. Rashi and Karo follow the T. without taking notice of the deviation. Kimchi noticed it in the T. Hitzig, Ehrlich and Krauss would read here מזי . (Com. Onk. Deut. 32, 34), which would, however, not agree with this rendering.

4) Kimchi seems to have noticed it. Though the absolute מלך is always rendered literally by the T. Com. Gray Is. In. Com. As to ובאלהיו see Dill P. Ehrlich IS.

5) Lxx P. omit כהרים מטה and have part of בהניף.

6) So Lxx P. In general the T. is apt to such an interchange, as will appear in the sequel.

7) So Lxx P. V. Kimchi also noticed it in the T. This reading of the T. was adopted by Hitz., Cheyne, Guthe and Kn.

	M. T.	Targ.	R.
IS. 29:13	יען כי נגש	חלף דאתרברב	נגש (1
`` 30:6	בארץ לביא וליש מהם אפעה ושרף מעופף	אתר דאריא בר אריון	מהם Vac.(2
`` 30:8	לעד עד עולם	לסהדו	לעד (3
`` 30:27	וכבד משאה	וקשי מלסוברא	וכבד משאה
`` 38:13	שויתי	אנחנא נחמית	שועתי
`` 40:6	וכל חסדו	וכל תוקפיהון	חסנו
`` 40:17	כל הגוים כאין נגדו מאפס ותהו נחשבו לו	כל עממיא כלמא עובריהון גמירא ושיצאה אינון חשיבין קדמוהי	אפס... נגדו Vac.(4
`` 43:4	ואתן אדם תחתיך ולאמים תחת נפשך	ומסרית עממיא תחותך ומלכותא חלף נפשך	ואתן עמים(5
`` 48:7	ולפני יום ולא שמעתם	ולא בסרתינון	שמעתים(6
`` 49:17	מהרו בניך	יוחון יבנון חרבתיך	בניך(7
`` 53:7	נגש והוא נענה	בעי	נגש(8
`` 54:9	כי מי נח זאת לי	כיומי דנח	כימי
`` 56:11	והמה רעים לא ידעו הבין	אינון מבאשין	רעים(9

1) So in many MSS. Com. Kimchi and Seder Eliahu r. 2, 24

2) Cort would have משם so Krauss, which would have the support of the T.; still, it is not improbable that the rendering is explanatory.

3) So P. V.

4) Lxx also omit נגדו ; Lxx and P. read לאפס. There is no reason to suppose that נגדו was omitted for anthropomorphical reasons.

5) This is suggester by the parallel; but it may also be explanatory. Graetz and Klost. amend איים which would have the support of the T.

6) Com. Lxx P. V.

7) So Lxx. (Com. San. 64b: וכל בניך אל תקרא בניך אלא בוניך).

8) So P. Sym. V. (See Dil. P. T. 2) and in many old Hebrew MSS. Com. Chayoth, Mebo Hatalmud, 25. Com. Berachoth 7b, 14a.

9) So Lxx P. and S. Kimchi remarks: ומן התימא שתרג׳ יונתן רעים מבאשין.

M. T.		Targ.	R.
``	58:3	וכל עצביכם תנגשון	אתון מקרבין	תנגשון 1)
``	59:18	כעל גמלות כעל ישלם	מרי גמליא	בעל נמולות 2)
``	61:3	מעטה תחלה תחת		
		רוח כהה	רוח משבחא חלף	רוח תהלה 3)
``	65:1	אל גוי לא קרא בשמי	דלא מצלי בישמי	קרא 4)
Jer.	6:14	וירפאו את שבר עמי	ואסיאו ית חבר	את שבר
			כנשתא דעמי	בת עמי 5)
``	10:24	יסרני אך במשפט	לא יתקף רוגזך	יסרם...
			בהון דלמא יזערון פן תמעיטני	ימעטו 6)
``	11:12	שמעו את דברי הברית	קבלו ית פתגמא	ודברתם 8)
		ודברתם אל איש יהודה	ותמלליגון 7)	
``	11:14	בעת קראם אלי בעד	בעידן דאת מצלי	קראך אלי
		רעתם	עליהון בעידן בישתהון	בעת רעתם 9)
``	15:14	והעברתי את איביך	ותשתעבדון וכו'	והעבדתי 10)
``	23:26	עת מתי היש בלב	עד אימתי אית	ער מתי יש 11)
		הנביאים	בלבהון	
``	27:8	עד תמי אתם בידו	עד דאמסר יתהון	עד תתי 12)

1) So Lxx. Kimchi: ומן התימה שתרגם אותו יונתן וכל תקלתכון מקרבין תרגם כמו בשין.

2) But Is. 63:7 כעל כל אשר literally.

3) It is possible to explain the rendering of the T. as suggested by the parallel רוח כהה, and would smoothen the difficulties felt by the commentators on this point.

4) So Lxx P.

5) They might, however, have been influenced by 8:11.

6) So Lxx. Com., however, chapter General Peculiarities.

7) So Lagarde. The same MS. was also before Kimchi, but in the copy of the Minchath Shai and many others the reading is ותמללון.

8) So Lxx. Com. P.

9) Lxx P. A. and many Hebrew MSS. Otherwise the T. might have been influenced by v. 12: והושע לא יושיעו להם בעת רעתם.

10) So Lxx P. Kimchi noticed it in the T. and remarks that he found this reading in many MSS. See also Kittel: Guesebrecht. Still, it is not impossible that the T. was influenced here by 17:4 והעבדתיך את איביך and hence the reading of the Lxx P.

11) So Lxx P.

12) So P.; also noticed by Giesbrecht and Cor., but it may also be interpretative.

	M. T.	Targ.	R.
" 29:12	ותצלון קדמי ואקבל וקראתם אתי והלכתם	וקראתם אתי
	צלותכון ותבעון מן והתפללתם אלי	ושמעתי אליכם[1]
	קדמי ואקבל בעותכון ושמעתי אליכם	
" 31:39	וכל השדמות	וכל אדייתא	וכל הזרמות[2]
" 49:3	והתשוטטנה בגדרות	ואתחמא בסיען	בגדרות[3]
" 51:3	אל ידרך... ואל יתעל	לא ימתח... ולא	אל ידרך[4]
Ez. 1:7	וכף רגליהם ככף רגל עגל	כפרסת רגלין סגלגלן	עגל[5]
" 5:11	וגם אני אגרע	ואף אנא אקטף תקף וכו'	אגרע[6]
" 7:5	רעה אחת רעה	בישתא בתר בישתא	אחר[7]
" 10:6	אשר תרתי לכם	דיהבית לכון	נתתי לכם[8]
" 10:29	אשר אתם הבאים שם	דאתון אתן	אשר אתם באים[9]
" 12:12	פניו יכסה יען אשר לא יראה לעין היא את הארץ	חלף דחב הוא ולא יחזי ית ארעא	יען אשר לא יראה לעון את הארין[10]

---

1) Probably הלכתם was omitted in the text of the T. P. also omits it. Lxx omits the entire portion and begins with והתהלכתם Giesb. conjecture ונעתרתי by the T. is not justified.

2) Lxx has here the Ketib. P. omits it entirely. The reading זרמות by the T. is the only plausible explanation of the peculiar rendering of this word. שדמות is usually rendered by the T. by מישרא נחלא (1K 23:4; IS. 16:1). Com. Aruch אדייתא and אורתא.

3) Felt by Kimchi. Com. P.

4) So Lxx codd. 88, 106, P. In some MSS. לא is the Keri. Felt by Minchat Shai and Kimchi.

5) So A. Rashi follows it.

6) So P. Sym. Vulg. This is the Ketib to Madnechai, but this reading is to be found in many MSS. So in M'turgom of Eliahu Halevy under root קטף. He cites this verse reading אגדע.

7) Noticed by Kimchi.

8) So P., so Toy. was probably influenced by V. 15.

9) So Lxx P.

10) So P. Probably both of them read לעין (Com. Is. 18:9 etc.). On the other hand, we find this case עין Ketib and עון Keri (Com. 2S 16:12).

		M. T.	Targ.	R.
"	13:11	ואתנה אבני אלגביש	וית אבני אלגביש	ואת אבני אנלביש[1]
"	13:21	את נפשים	ית נפשיהון	נפשם
"	14:8	ונחמתם על הרעה	על כל בישתא	על כל[2]
"	14:22	מברחיו	גבורוהי	מבחריו[3]
"	16:15	והשמותיהו	ואשויניה	והשימותיהו[4]
"	16:36	ותשפכי את זנותיך ולא כשר לך למעבד על כל עובר לו יהי	כך	לא יהי[5]
"	17:21	ובדמי בניך אשר נתתי להם	ובחובת דם בנך	ובדמי בניך[6]
"	18:17	מעני השיב ידו	ממסכנא לא אתיב ידיה	מעני לא השיב[7]
"	19:7	וידע אלמנותיו	ואצרי בירניתיה	וירע ארמנותיו[8]
"	21:19	חרב החדרת להם	רמזיעא להון	החרדת[9]
"	21:21	התאחדי הימיני	אשתליפי וכו'	התחדי[10]
"	21:21	השימי	ושיצי	בשין

---

1) Minchat Shai: נראה שהיה קורא ואת אבני אלגביש ;ויונתן... Kimchi remarks that he found this reading in a MS.

2) So in some MSS. Caro l. c.

3) So Lxx, Syro Hex. and in five MSS. of Kenn. and De Rossi.

4) Noticed by Rashi and Kimchi; so also in Ald. Codd. 42, 68.

5) So P. and in some De Rossi MSS.

6) So P. and Vulg. and a great number of MSS.; the Afudi, ch. 14, remarks: באה חכף תמורת הבית בארבע רוחות השמים (זכריה ב') כרוח קדים (ירמיה י"ח, י"ז) באשר ילבי (הושע ז', י"ב) כדמי בניך.

7) Probably interpretative, making the following לא referring to מעני; also Lxx; so 28th middah of R. Eliezer. See Eliezer of Beaugency, who puts as an explanation of עול מעני. Com. Heller על התר' הירוש.

8) So A. aliter et dimit palatium eorum. So EW. Toy וירע Com. Kimchi. His point, however, is not clear. The T. rendering of Jud. 8:16 ויודע is ותבב or וגבר as Kimchi had it or גרר as in Lag. or ואלקי as cited in בחן אבן by Menachem b. Solomon.

9) So Lxx P. A. Vulg. was noticed also by Kimchi.

10) So is rendered הוחדה (v. 15). John d. Buch Ez. assumes it represents a Syr. Ith. form.

		M. T.	Targ.	R.
``	24:26	בא הפליט אליך להשמעות אזנים	לאשמעותיך בסורא	להשמעותך [1]
``	26:2	אמלאה החרבה	דהות מליא חרובה	המלאה אמלאה [2]
``	26:20	כחרבות	בחרבתא	בחרבות [3]
``	27:6	בת אשרים	רפין דאשכדעין	בתאשר [4]
``	27:23	ונתתי יארים חרבה	ואתן נהריהון	יאריהם
``	30:12	אשור בלמד	אתור ומדי	כל מדי
``	34:26	ונתתי אתם וסביבות גבעתי	ואשרי יתהון סחור סחור	סביבות
``	39:16	וגם שם עיר המונה	ואף לתמן	שם
Hos. 4:18	סר סבאם	שלטוניהון אסגיאו	שר [5]
``	6:5	ומשפטיך אור יצא	ודיני בנהור נפיק	ומשפטי כאור יצא [6]
``	7:12	כשמע לעדתם	על דשמעו לעצתהון	עדותם [7]
``	8:5	זנח עגלך שמרון	טעו בתר עגלא	זנח [8]
``	9:1	אל תשמח ישראל אל גיל בעמים	לא תחדון ולא תביעון	ואל גיל [9]
``	11:7	ואל על יקראהו	תערערון	יקראו [10]
``	12:1	ויהודה עוד רד עם אל ועם קדושים נאמן	עד דגלא עמא דאלהא, ואינון רהוו פלחין קדמי מתקרן עמא קדישא	עם אל... ועם קרושים [11]
``	13:10	אהי מלכך	...אן	איה [12]

---

1) So Lxx P.

2) So Lxx; accepted by Co. Seeg. Gratz.

3) So Lxx P.

4) Com. Is. 41:19. Felt by Kimchi.

5) Felt by Kimchi.

6) So Lxx P. (Com. Nowack Die Kl. P.).

7) So Lxx P. רעתב (See Vollers Z. A. T. W., 1883, 250).

8) So P.

9) So Lxx P.

10) So P.

11) So Lxx P. Kimchi: ומן התומה שת״י עם אל כמו עם אל בפתח.

12) So Lxx P.

	M. T.	Targ.	R.
Am. 5:10	ושד על מבצר יבוא	ובזוזין... משליט	יביא (1
" 6:10	ומסרפו	מיקידא	מסרפו
Mi. 4:9	עתה למה תריעי רע	וכען למה את מתחברא	תרע רע (2
" 6:11	האזכה במאזני רשע	היזכון	היזבח (3
Nahum 2:3	כגאון ישראל	רבותיה לישראל	גאון
" 3:6	כראי	לעיני כל חזך	לראי (4
Zef. 3:18	אספתי ממך היו	... וי עליהון...	הוי
Ze. 9:13	ועוררתי בניך ציון על בניך יון	ואגבר בנך ציון	ועודרתי (5
" 12:5	אמצה לי ישב ירושלם	אשתכח פרקן ליתבי ירושלם	אמצא ליושבי ירושלם (6
" 14:5	ונסתם גיא הרי	ויסתתים	ונסתם (7
" 14:6	לא יהיה אור יקרות וקפאין	לא יהי נהורא אלהין ערי וגליד	וקרות (8
Mal. 2:5	ואתנם לו מורא	ויהבית	ואתן (9

1) So in some MSS. and Lxx P.

2) So Lxx, though in a different sense.

3) So Lxx P.

4) So Lxx P.

5) (Is. 14:9) עורר לך רפאים : וויחי עלוהי (Is. 10:26) ועורר עליו אעירת.

6) The reading of the T. was probably אמצא found in many MSS. See Min. Shai.

7) So Sym. Ald. Codd. III, XII, 22, 23, 26. De Rossi found this reading in the Lxx. וכן נמצא במקצת ספרים Kimchi. So Kimchi ספר השרשים; also R. Eliah Halevy הגהת השרשים and Ibn Ezra pointing out this being the reading of אנשי המזרח. Com. Eich. Ein. V. 1, p. 419 (German Ed. 1787).

8) But com. Gen. 42:9 etc. See Rikmah on the change of Waw to Jod. Com. Sup. Am. 5:10.

9) So Lxx P.

GROUP B

	M. T.	Targ.	Following
Joshua 7:8	הפך ישראל ערף	קדלהון	אויביו [1]
" 8:14	והוא לא ידע כי ארב לו	ואינון לא ידעון ארי כמנא להון	וימהרו וישכימו וירוצו [2]
" 9:20	והחיה אותם	ונקים	זאת נעשה [3]
" 20:5	כי בבלי דעת	בלא מדעיה	הכה את רעהו
Judges 2:14	ביד שסים	בוזזיהון	ביד אויביהם לפני אויביהם
" 2:22	את דרך	אורחן דתקנ...	ללכת בם [4]
" 20:37	והאורב החישו ויפשטו	אוחי ואתנגד	וימשך האורב ויך [5]
1S. 2:29	להבריאכם	לאוכלותהון	Implied [6]
" 6:4	כי מגפה אחת לכלם	לכולכון	ולסרניכם [7]
" 17:40	בכלי הרעים	ובתרמיליה	אשר לו וקלעו [8]
2S. 3:15	מעם איש	מלות בעלה	ויקחה [9]
" 23:5	וכל חפץ	וכל בעותי	כי כל ישעי [10]
1K. 8:46	לפני אויב	בעלי דבביהון	ונתתם בעזבכם
" 18:18	ותלך	ואזלתון	אשר שלחה
" 21:11	כאשר כתוב	כמא דכתבת	את הספרים
2K. 19:4	ויפרשהו	ופרסינון	אשר נתנו
" 23:5	ויקטר	ואסיקו	
IS 10:8	מנפש ועד בשר	נפשיהון עם פגריהון	יערו וכרמלו [11]
" 13:2	ויבא פתחי נדיבים	ויעלון בתרעהא	implied by context [12]
" 19:20	מפני לחצים	דחקיהון	וישלח להם... והצילם [13]

1) Also v. 12; so P.
2) Lxx put the whole in singular. So P.
3) So P.
4) Sbirin, followed by Lxx Lag. So P.
5) So Lxx P.
6) So P.
7) So P.
8) So P.
9) So Lxx P.
10) So P.
11) P. has it in the 2nd person. Com. Lxx.
12) P. in 2 p. f.
13) So Lxx.

	M. T.	Targ.	Following
" 21:14	בלחמו	לחמא דאתון אכלין	התיו
" 23:13	בחניו	חזותהא	ארמנתיה
" 26:8	אף ארח משפטיך קוינוך לשמך ולזכרך תאות נפש	לארח דינך סברנא לשמך ולדוכרנך תאות נפשנא	קוינוך 1)
" 26:9	נפשי אויתך... אף רוחי בקרבי אשחרך	נפשי מחמדא אף רוחי... מברכא לך	נפשי... רוחי 2)
" 26:19	יחיו מתיך נבלתי יקומון	גרמי נבלתהון	הקיצו ורננו 3)
" 30:11	סורו מני דרך הטו מני אורח	אסטיונא... אבטלונא	השביתו מפנינו 4)
" 30:13	בחומה נשגבה	כשור מתקף	כפרין נפל
" 33:2	היה זרעם לבקרים אף ישועתנו בעת צרה	הוי תוקפנא... אף פורקננא	חננו... קוינו... ישועתנו 5)
" 33:3	מרוממתך נפצו גוים ורותה ארצם מרם	מסני נבורן איתבדרו מלכותא	מקול המון 6)
" 34:7	ועפרם מחלב ידשן	ותרוי ארעהון מדמהון ועפרהון מתרבהון ידהן	ורותה ארצם ועפרם 7)
" 40:26	לכלם בשם יקרא	בשמהן	צבאם 8)
" 44:7	הבאתיו והצליח דרכו	ואצליחת	הבאתיו 9)
" 46:1	נשאתיכם	מטולי טעותהון	היו עצביהם

1) So P. Lxx. Rashi, Kimchi, Karo fellow this explanation.

2) So P.

3) So P.

4) So Lxx (see the difficult explanations of Kimchi).

5) So P.

6) P. puts for the same purpose המון in the 2nd p.

7) So Lxx. P. in מחלב only.

8) Lxx P. render in pl., influenced by Ps. 147:5.

9) So Lxx P.

	M. T.	Targ.	Following
`` 42:6	ולא יכלו מלט משא	נטליהון	ונפשם
`` 48:15	ומי כמוני יקרא	ומן כותי דין ערעינה	ויגדה ויערכה [1]
`` 51:8	כי בבגד יאכלם עש וכצמר יאכלם סם	ארי כלבושא דאכיל ליה עשא וכעמרא דאחיד ביה רוקבא	כבגד... כצמר [2]
`` 57:15	מרום וקדוש אשכן	ברומא שרי וקדישא שכינתה	וקדוש שמו [3]
`` 58:14	והרכבתיך... והאכלתיך	וישרינך... ויוכלינך	implied by context
Jer. 2:27	אומרים לעץ אבי אתה	אבונא את	ילדתנו
`` 7:24	במעצות	בעצתיהון	בשרירות לבם
`` 9:6	שבתך בתוך מרמה	יתבין בבית כנשתהון	במרמה מאנו
`` 10:4	במסמרות ובמקבות יחזקום	מתקיף ליה	ייפהו
`` 11:14	בעת קראם	בעידן ראת מצלי	אל תתפלל
`` 11:22	הבחורים ימותו בחרב בניהם ובנותיהם ימתו ברעב	עולמיהון יתקטלון	בניהם ובנותיהם [4]
Ez. 11:19	ונתתי להם לב אחד		
`` 11:22	ורוח חדשה... בקרבכם	ורוח דחילא אתן במעיהון	ונתתי להם [5]
`` 22:10	ערות אב גלה	גליאו	ענו בך [6]
`` 22:30	ועשתה גלולים עליה	בנוה	שפכת דם בתוכה

---

1) Lxx P. render them all in absolute.
2) So P.
3) So P. Lxx seem to have had an entirely different reading.
4) So Lxx.
5) So Lxx P. Sym. Vul.
6) So Lxx Sym.

	M. T.	Targ·	
" 23:40	ואף כי תשלחנה	ארי שלחת	רחצת כחלת... ועדית
" 26:11	לארץ תרד	ימגר	ירמס... יהרג הריו
" 35:8	גבעותיך וגיאותיך וכל אפיקיך	ית רמתוהי וחילוהי וכל פצידוהי	הריו
" 35:10	שתי הארצות לי תהיינה וירשנוה	וארתינון	שתי הארצות[1]
" 36:20	ויבוא אל הגוים אשר באו שם	ועלו לביני עממיא	אשר באו[2]
	כאשר שממו עליך	ותארו כמה דסברו ליה	מראהו...
Hos. 10:1	כרב לפריו הרבה למזבחותיו כטוב לארצו הטיבו מצבות	אסניאו פולחן לאגוריהון... קמתהון	לפריו... לארצו[3]
" 14:9	פריך	לתיובתהון	ואשורגו
Am. 2:3	והכרתי שופט	דינהא	וכל שריה
Mi. 5:4	עליו	עלנא	בארצנו... בארמנותינו... והקמנו
" 7:15	כימי צאתך	מפקהון	אראגו
Na. 2:14	רכבה	רתיכך	וכפיריך
" 3:7	מי ינוד לה	מן ידוי עלך	מנחמים לך[4]
Za. 14:5	ובא יהוה אלהי כל קדושים עמך	עמיה	ובא[5]

---

1) It is not necessary with Cor. (D. B. Ez.) to suppose a different reading by the T. Suggested by the text, the T. would not hesitate to render it as if it were in Hiph.

2) So P.; so also in Ez. 20:38; 23:44; Jerem. 51:36; Mi. 7:12, noticed by Min. Shai. In Masoreth Seder Sh'lach this is considered among those that are written in sing. and the Sebirin in pl. That the T. follows in a good many cases the Sebirin as well as the Mad-nechai was noticed by the Min Shai. (Com. Ez. 5:11; 13:17; 14:19; Min. Shai Jerem. 49:36; Mi. 7:12). In P'sichta Lam r. לא היה צריך קרא ...למימר אלא ויבואו אלא כביכול. So in many Kenn. MSS.

3) Lxx make למזבחות conform to מצבות. P. follows it closely.

4) So P. Lxx put all in the 3rd person. The reading of לך is found in many MSS.

5) So Lxx P. noticed also by Kimchi.

	M. T.	Targ.	Following
Mal. 2:15	ובאשת נעוריך אל יבגד	... לא תשקר	ונשמרתם [1]
" 2:16	כי שנא שלח... וכסה חמס על לבושו	ולא תכסי חטאה בלבושך	ברוחכם... תבגדו [2]

GROUP C

לא תדחל ולא תתבר Targum אל תערץ ואל תחת Joshua 1:9
לא תדחל ולא תתבר On. לא תירא ולא תחת According to Deut. 31:8

ואטמרתנון [3] Targum ותצפנו Joshua 2:4 . According to v. 6
ותטמנם .

ית ארון קימא דייי [4] Targum שאו את ארון הברית Joshua 6:6 .
וארון ברית יהוה According to v. 8 .

קדם ארונא דייי [5] Targum לפני יהוה Joshua 6:8 . According
לפני ארון יהוה to v. 7 .

ואזדודו [6] Targum ויצטירו Joshua 9:4 . According to v. 12
הצטידנו .

ובמשפך מרמתא Targum ובאשדות Joshua 12:8 . According
אשדות הפסגה to 12:13 .

מתנן די יהב להון אינון Targum בהנת יהוה נחלתו Joshua 18:7
— יהוה אלהי ישראל הוא נחלתם According to 13:33 אחסנתהון
מתנן די יהב להון... .

לית לכון חולק Targum מה לכם ולי/ אלהי ישראל Joshua 22:24
במימרא . According to vv. 25, 27 ...אין לכם חלק. .

כד אתרעיאו בני ישראל Targum יבחר אלהים חדשים Judges 5:8
למפלח לטעותא חדתין דמקרב אתעבידא דלא איתעסקו בהון אבהתכון.
According to Deut. 32:17 אלהים חדשים מקרוב באו ולא שערום
אבתיכם .

---

1) So Lxx.

2) So Lxx.

3) Lxx in both places have ἔκρυψεν Com. Jalqut l. c.

4) So P.

5) So P. V. and 4 MSS. and in 3 Kenn.

6) Many Kenn. and De Rossi MSS. read ויצטידו . So Lxx P.
Felt by Kimchi

דשדן בידיהון [1] Targum בשלשת מאות האיש המלקקים Judges 7:7
. לפומהון . According to v. 6 ויהי מספר המלקקים אל פיהם

חרבא דמקטלא [2] Targum ואמרתם ליהוה ולגדעון Judges 7:18
. מן קדם . According to v. 20 ויקראו חרב לי' ולגדעון

יטור דתנן [3] Targum משאת העשן . According
to v. 40 ...יטור — עמור העשן

והא סליק Targum והנה עלה כליל העיר השמימה Judges 20:40
והנה עלה עשן According to Joshua 8:20 . תננא דקרתא לצית שמיא
. והא סליק תננא — העיר השמימה

על... Targum והנה עלי ישב על הכסא יד דרך מצפה 1S 4:13
על כבש אורח — בעד השער According to v. 18 . כביש אורח תרעא [4]
. תרעא

ודמית חמוהא ודאתקטל [5] Targum ואל חמיה ואישה 1S 4:21
ודמית חמוהא — ומת חמיה ואישה According to v. 19 . בעלה
. ודאתקטל בעלה

ועד אבנא רבתא [6] Targum ועד אבל הגדולה 1S 6:18 . According to vv. 14, 15   האבן הגדולה .

המון משרית פלשתאי [7] Targum והנה ההמון נמוג 1S 14:16 .
According to v. 19   וההמון אשר במחנה פלשתים

לשבחא בחנגיא Targum לשיר והמחלות . According to
21:12   יענו במחולות — משבחין בחנגיא . [8]

האית עוד גברא [9] Targum האפס עוד איש לבית שאול 2S 9:3 .
According to v. 1   האית — הכי יש עוד .

לקי בתרתין רגלוהי Targum נכה רגלים 2S 9:3 . According to
v. 13   לקי בתרתין רגלוהי — והוא פסח שתי רגליו .

___

1) So P. In some MSS. of the T. the words בידיהון לפומהון
are omitted

2) So P. In Lag. דמקטלא is omitted.

3) P. omits משאת .

4) So Lxx. Kimchi: ויונתן הוסיף בו שער שתרגם על כבש אורח
תרעא מסכי כמו שאמר בפסוק האחר בעד יד השער .

5) Com. Lxx.

6) So Lxx and many MSS.

7) So Lxx P.

8) In Lag. משמעין .

9) So Lxx P. Kimchi: ותמהתי למה תרגמו יונתן האית .

2S 11:6 וישלח יואב את אוריה אל דוד Targum (1 ית אוריה חתאה.
את אוריה החתי According to the preceding.

According. Targum (2 בעבור הילד חי 2S 12:21 ער דרביא קים.
בעוד הילד חי to v. 22.

According to. Targum (3 עיר המים 2S 12:27 קרית מלכותא.
עיר המלוכה v. 26.

2S 15:17 ויצא המלך וכל העם Targum ונפק מלכא וכל אנשי
ביתיה. (4 Accordnig to v. 16 וכל אנש ביתיה — ויצא המלך וכל ביתו.

2S 18:12 שמרו מי בנער Targum בעולימא לי אסתמרו.
According to v. 5 לאט לי לנער — בעולימא לי אסתמרו.

2S 22:13 מננה נגדו בערו גחלי אש Targum דנור כגומרין.
מימריה דלקא According to v. 9 (5 נחלים בערו ממנו — דנור כגומרין.
מימריה דלקא.

1K 1:48 אשר נתן היום יושב על כסאי Targum (6 דין יומא דיהב.
בר יתיב על כורסי According to 3:6... ותתן לי בן ישב.

According. Targum (7 לא יפל משערתו 1K 1:52 דרישיה משער.
אם יפול משערת ראשו to 1S 14:45.

1K 9:8 והבית הזה יהיה עליון Targum (8 עילאי דהוה הדין וביתא.
יהי חרוב According to 2 Ch. 7:21 לכל עליון היה אשר הזה והבית.
עובר עליו ישם...

1K 12:16 מה לנו חלק בדוד Targum לנא לית (9 According to.
2S 20:1 אין לנו חלק בדוד.

1K 13:9 ולא תשתה מים תמן מיא (10 Targum ולא תשתי. Accord-
ולא תשתה שם מים ing to v. 17.

1K 13:34 ויהי בדבר הזה לחטאת Targum והוה פתגמא הדין.
ויהי הדבר הזה לחטאת According to 12:13.

1K 22:31 ומלך ארם צוה את שרי הרכב שלשים ושנים Targum
מלכון ותרין תלתין. (11. According to 20:16 שלשים ושנים מלך.

1)   So P. and in 2 MSS. Kenn.
2)   So Lxx P. Com. Ehrlich, Randglossen.
3)   So P. and in 2 MSS. Kenn.
4)   In Lag. וכל עמא.
5)   So Lxx P.
6)   So P. Lag. ἔδωκε σήμερον ἐκ τοῦ σπερυματος μοῦ
7)   So is the T. to 2S 14:11 משערת בנך, So P. here and in
2S 14:11. Lxx here only.
8)   Com. P.
9)   In Lag. מאלנא.
10)   In Lag. תמן is omitted.
11)   Literally in Lag.

According . סבהי אוביליה Targum (1 שאהו אל אמו 2K 4:19
וישאהו ויבאהו . to v. 20

According to . מארע דרומא Targum מבעל שלשה 2K 4:42
1S 9:4 בא. בארע דרומא — בארץ שלשה

According . השלם (2 Targum כה אמר המלך שלום 2K 9:19
to v. 18 . כה אמר המלך השלום

אתו לותי (3 Targum מארץ רחוקה באו מבבל 2K 20:14 .
According to . ומאין יבואו אליך

ואתקבר בגן עזא (4 Targum ויקבר בגן ביתו בגן עזא 2K 21:18 .
According to v. 26 . בגן עזא

וכל אנש Targum וכל איש יהודה וכל ישבי ירושלם 2K 23:2
וכל איש יהודה וישבי . According to 2 Ch. 34:3 יהודה ויתבי ירושלם
ירושלם .

ברם על דארגזי קדם י' (5 Targum אך על פי י' 2K 24:3 .
According to v. 20 . כי על אף

According . לא בחים Targum ולהכרית גוים לא מעט IS. 10:7
to Hab. 1:17 . לאספא עממין לא בחים — להרג גוים לא יחמול

וישתארון ביה Targum ונשאר בו עללות כנקף זית IS. 17:6
עוללין כביעור זיתא... כן ישתארו יחידאין צדיקיא בגו עלמא בין מלכותא .
According to 24:13 כי כה יהיה בקרב הארץ בתוך העמים כנקף זית
— ...ארי כדין ישתארון יחידאין צדיקיא .

כל ראשתכח ביך יתקטל (6 Targum כל נמצאיך אסרו יחדו IS. 22:3 .
According to 13:15 כל די ישתכח בה יתקטל — כל הנמצא ירקר .

בעדנא ההיא ישבחון Targum ביום ההוא יושר השיר הזה IS. 26:1
תושבחתא חדתא (7 According to 42:10 שירו לי' שיר חדש .

האפשר דיימר טינא Targum כי יאמר מעשה לעשהו IS. 29:16
לעבריה . According to 45:9 היאמר חמר ליצרו .

_____

1) So P. Com Lxx.
2) Com. P. Lxx εἰ εἰϱηνη
3) So Lxx P. לותי is omitted in Lag.
4) Com. Lxx. Both are rendered in Lag.
5) So Lxx. Com. P.
6) The whole phrase is omitted in Lxx and P.
7) In Lag. הדא .

בריל עובדיכון בישיא Targum רוחכם אש תאכלכם IS. 33:11
— וסערה כקש תשאם 40:24 According to . מימרי בעלעולא לקשא
. ומימריה בעלעולא לקשא1)

IS. 41:4 מי פעל ועשה קרא הדרות מראש אני יהוה ראשון ואת
מן אמר אילין קים אמר ועביד... אנא ברית 2)Targumאחרונים אני הוא
. עלמא מבראשית ואף עלמי עלמיא דילי אינון בר מני לית אלהא
According to 44:6 — אני ראשון ואני אחרון ומבלעדי אין אלהים
. אנא הוא דמלקדמון אף עלמי עלמיא...3)

IS. 42:18 רשיעיא דאינון כחרשין הלא Targum החרשים שמעו
. וחרשים ואזנים למו 43:8 According to . אודנין לכון שמעו

. ובמקובין מתקיף ליה Targum ובמקבות יצרהו IS. 44:12
According to Jer. 10:4 ובמקבות יחזקום4) — ובמכבין מתקיף ליה .

. לא עבדתני Targum היאמר חמר ליצרו מה תעשה IS. 45:9
According to 29:16 . כי יאמר מעשה לעשהו לא עשני .

. לעלם אחי תקיפת מלכו Targum לעולם אהיה גברת IS. 47:7
According to v. 5 תקיפת מלכון — לא תוסיפי יקראו לך גברת ממלכות .

IS. 50:8 קריבא זכותי Targum קרוב מצדיקי . According to
51:5 קריבא זכותי — קרוב צדקי .

IS. 63:5 ואביט ואין עזר ואשתומם ואין סומך ותושע לי זרעי
וידיע קדמי ולית איש דיקום ויבעי עליהון Targum וחמתי היא סמכתני
According to . ופרקתינון בדרע תוקפי ובמימר רעותי סעדתינון
59:16 וידיע קדמוהי ולית אנש דיקום — וישתומם כי אין מפגיע
. ויבעי עליהון ופרקינון בדרע תוקפיה ובמימר רעותיה סעדינון

Jer. 6:11 לאיתי לסוברא Targum ואת חמת יהוה נלאיתי הכיל
— ונלאיתי כלכל לא אוכל 20:9 According to . ולא יבילית למשפך
. ולאיתי לסוברא ולא יבילית .

Jer. 8:15 סברנא לשלם Targum קוה לשלום . According to
14:19 סברנא לשלם — מדוע הכיתנו...

---

1) It renders this way Is. 41:16: וסערה תפיץ אותם — ומימריה
כעלעולא לקשא . In Lag. לקשא is omitted.

2) So the T. renders Is. 40:12, seemingly for their similar beginning and contents.

3) So, for the same reason, it renders 43:10: כי אני הוא לפני
. אנא הוא דמלקדמין... — לא נוצר אל

4) See Jerem. 10:4. The rendering there was influenced by the
sequel, but the influence in this case might have been reciprocal, so
that the v. was put in the same p. in accordance with the verse here.

Jer. 10:4 בכספא ובדהבא חפי ליה Targum בכסף ובזהב ייפהו.
According to Is. 40:19 ¹)ירקענו בזהב וצרף — ליה מחפי.

Jer. 10:4 דלא יצטלי Targum ולא יפיק. According to Is.
40:20, 41:7 ²)ימט לא — יצטלי דלא.

Jer. 30:15 ממרעא מחתיך Targum אנוש מכאבך. According
to v. 12 מכתך נחלה — מחתיך ממרעא.

Jer. 31:9 ברחמין סגיאין Targum בבכי יבאו ובתחנונים אוביליס
וברחמין — וברחמים גדולים אקבצך. According to Is. 54:7 אקרבינון
סגיאין אקרב.

Jer. 32:35 דלא פקדית Targum אשר לא צויתים ולא עלתה על לבי
אשר לא צויתי ולא עלתה על לבי ³). According to 7:31 באורייתי
— דלא פקדית באורייתי.

Jer. 33:3 רברבן ונטירן Targum ואגידה לך גדולות ובצרות
וגטירן — ונצרות ולא ידעתם ⁴). According to Is. 48:6.

Jer. 41:15 ואזל למיעבר ליה Targum וילך אל בני עמון
וילך לעבר אל בני עמון. According to v. 10 בני עמון.

Jer. 46:8 אחפי ארעא ומלאה Targum אעלה אכסה ארץ
ויבזון ארעא ומלאה — וישטפו ארץ ומלואה. According to 47:2.

Jer. 48:4 איתברת מלכות מואב Targum נשברה מואב. According to 48:25 מלכות מואב — נגדעה קרן מואב.

Ez. 11:19 ונתתי להם לב אחד ורוח חדשה אתן בקרבם Targum
ואתן לכון — לב חדש. According to 36:26 ⁵)ואתן להון לב דחיל
לב דחיל.

---

1) So P. Rashi; Kimchi etc. curiously combine both readings.
F. Perles in J. Q. R., v. 18, p. 388, would read here יצפהו and refers
to Is. 30:22; so Kittel, both of whom refer to the T. not appreciating
the principle followed in this case. So also in Jerem. 10:19, and
curiously enough, P. there renders ירקענו in the same way as ויופהו.

2) So Lxx, except in Is. 40:20.

3) Lxx read there צויתים as here.

4) Minchat Shai sees another reading by the T. and goes so far
as to think that Rashi, who follows the T., has also had the same
reading. But Rashi does it in numerous instances where such an assumption is out of question. Kimchi remarks: וי"ת רברבן ונטירן, היה
קורא ונצורות בנו"ן.

5) Also 18:31. So P., felt by Minchat Shai. Curiously, this reading appears also in the com. of Eliezer of Beaugency (published by
Posnansky, 213). So is the reading in 3 Kenn. MSS. and 1 De Rossi.

Ez. 17:5 ויהביה בחקל טוב Targum ויתנהו בשדה זרע. According
ing to v. 8 (1 בחקל טוב — אל שדה טוב.

Ez. 29:3 דילי מלכותא ואנא Targum לי יארי ואני עשיתני.
מלכותא — יאר לי ואני עשיתי (2. According to v. 9 כבשית
דילי ואנא כבשית.

Ez. 29:6 סמך קניא רעיעא Targum יען היותם משענת קנה.
According to Is. 36:6 סמך קניא רעיעא — הקנה הרצוץ.

Ez. 30:18 כעננא דסליק וחפי ית Targum היא ענן יכסנה.
ארעא. According to 38:16 (3 כעננא — כענן לכסות הארץ.
דסליק וחפי ית ארעא.

Ez. 31:14 עם נחתי גוב בית אבדנא Targum אל יורדי בור.
According to 32:18, 24 את יורדי בור.

Ez. 31:15 ביום אחתותי Targum ביום רדתו שאולה. According to v. 16 באחתותהי יתיה — בהורידי אתו שאלה.

Ez. 32:5 ויתמלון חיליא Targum ומלאתי הגיאיות. According
to v. 6 (4 יתמלון — ואפקים ימלאון.

Ez. 32:18 לארעא ארעיתא Targum אל ארץ תחתיות. According to 31:14 (5 לארעא ארעיתא — אל ארץ תחתית.

Ez. 32:24 דאיתמסירו לתבר Targum אשר נתנו חתיתם. According to v. 23 אשר נתנו חתית.

Ez. 34:24 ועבדי דוד מלכא (6 Targum ועבדי דוד נשיא בתוכם.
According to 37:24 ועבדי דוד מלך עליהם.

Ez. 36:12 ואסגי עליבון (7 Targum והולכתי עליכם אדם.
According to vv. 10, 11 ואסגי עליבון — והרביתי עליכם אדם.

Ez. 41:17 עד לעילא Targum על מעל הפתח. According
to v. 20 מהארץ עד מעל הפתח.

---

1) As to the change in person, com. De Rossi V. L. V. T., l. c.

2) P. reads יאר ; Lxx have v. 9 as in v. 3.

3) It also influenced Jer. 46:8.

4) Lxx have in v. 6 as in v. 5. Kittel wonders if the reading
was not ונמלאו.

5) So 26:20 בארץ תחתית.

6) Lxx have in 37:24 as in 34:24. Lag has here רבא.
However, in 37:25 the T. stands alone.

7) Ehrlich Ez. finds support in this rendering of the T. that it
is used here in the sense of increase, as in Jerem. 12:2. Equally wrong
is Jahn, ascribing a different reading to the T.

Ez. 43:10 וימשחון ית טקוסיה Targum ומרדו את תכנית .
According to v. 11 [1] צורת הבית ותכונתו .

Mi. 2:8 ממון יקרהון מנהון Targum ממול שלמה אדר תפשיטון
ממון יקרהון — ועורם מעליהם הפשיטו. According to 3:3 נסבין
מנהון נסכין [2] .

Ze. 3:10 לתחות פרי Targum אל תחת גפן ואל תחת תאנה
איש תחת גפנו According to 1K 5:5 . גופנוהי ולתחות פרי·תינוהי
ותחת תאנתו .

Ze. 9:8 ואשרי בבית מקרשי... Targum וחניתי לבית מצבה
ואני אהיה According to 2:9 . כשור ראשא מוקף לה סחור סחור
כשור ראשא מקף לה סחור סחור — לה חומת אש .

Ze. 11:17 וי על פרנסא טפשא Targum הוי רעי האליל .
According to v. 15 פרנסא טפשא — רעה אוילי .

---

1) So P.

2) Lxx read in 2:8 עור as in 33. So P.

THE EXEGESIS IN JONATHAN

The exegetical nature of T. Jonathan is in a conspicuous manner emphasized in the report of the Talmud : 'Said R. Jeremia, others say R. Hiyya b. Abba, Targum to the Prophets Jonathan b. Uziel said it. And Eretz Israel trembled 400 parasangs. A Bath Kol said: Who is the one who revealeth my mysteries to the children of men? Rose Jonathan b. Uziel and said: I am the one who revealeth Thy mysteries to the children of men. It is reavealed and known unto you that . . . I did it for Thy sake in order that strife may not abound in Israel." To the question why no such occurrence accompanied the act of the Targum to the Pentateuch, the answer is given: "The Pentateuch is clear while the Prophets contain things some of which are clear, while others are obscure." [1]

Framed as this report is in the characteristic phraseology of the Agada it serves not only to demonstrate the prevalent view of the age as to the principal characteristic of the T. to the Prophets, its main value resting in the exegesis, but is instructive also in that it manifests the worshipful reverence in which the exegesis was held. It was regarded as mysteries which should not, except for a weighty reason as alleged by Jonathan, he disclosed to the uninitiated in holiness. It does, however, in no way indicate the nature of the exegesis. There is nothing of the mystical in it. It is governed by rules and based on principles of a kind placing it in the domain of logical hermeneutics.

The general underlying principle in the exegesis of T. Jonathan consists in an attempt to render intelligible to the fullest possible degree that which is obscure. To accomplish this the targumist does not resort to the undersense. It is the sense, the explicit and simple, which is fundamental in the exege-

---

1) Meg. 3a; Yerushalmi 1, 10.

sis. The object of the targumist was to translate the poetical mind of the Prophet into the lay-mind behind it. In other words, to the targumist the implication rather than the surface literalness of the passage or word involved is of chief consideration. It is, on the one hand, a desire to correctly understand the prophet,[2] and on the other hand, to make the author intelligible to others.[3] Passages which are untouched by the exegesis of the targumist, the reason is to be sought in the assumption that the passage in question was not obscure to the generation of the targumist. In determining the general nature of the exegesis of this Targum a few salient points call for recording at the outset. In the first place, the targumist in no way dismisses any passage or word unrendered due to its embarrassing nature as is frequently the case in the Lxx and P. Whether or not the targumist is assured of having found a plausible escape or is resorting to some hopelessly obscure paraphrase, he is not evading it. On the other hand, it should be noticed that the T. appears entirely unaffected in his translation. He is not preoccupied with any particular thought, or hypothetical idea, "which assumes a connection in the train of thought which does not appear on the surface", as was the case with the Agada, Philo and the Church Fathers.[4] The aim he set for himself was translation; nothing beyond it. The targumist is inclined, however, in certain cases to parallelism of circumstances, as is the case with the Agada.

One thing, however, stands forth as peculiarly remarkable. It would appear the targumist had little regard for the historical reality of the prediction. With few exceptions he manifests no interest in the particular historical period or event of the prophecy. There is a strong inclination on the part of the targumist to shift the predicted reality to the Messianic age whenever the contents admit of such a presentation. He is this way interpreting the prophecies of "consola-

---

2) Com. Scheleiermacher, Hermenutik, etc. (ed. 1838), p. 3.

3) Immer, Hermenentik (ed. 1877), p. 10.

4) The case with the Agada needs no illustration. It constitutes one of its fundamental bases (com. particularly Maimonides preface to Seder Zerai'm end 2nd part). As to the Apostles, com. Epistle of James 2:21; Rom. 10:17.

tion" which his age of national depression and political de-
jection would hardly regard as already accomplished.[5]
In addition, there is the poetical side of the prophecy, its
overflowing richness of expression and exuberance of color in
portrayal which are not susceptible of realization, but which
were, in the belief of the people, unaware of this fact, to be
inevitably translated into reality. Hence the tendency to
interpret the glowing description of the "consolation" in
Messianic terms.[6]   The Messianic tone is made audible
also in the prominence given in his exegesis to the
"righteous ones". In a good many instances no other reason
except to give Messianic sense to a phrase, is evident.[7]   But
of significance is also the introduction of the wicked side by
side with the righteous.   In this way the M e s s i a n i c
description is complete. The Messianic epoch, as is generally
known, is in its final form rather religious and individual than
political, national. The righteous and the wicked, not the nation and nations, are the object of its justice. Finally, the
Messianic tendency has found its expression in the targumist
references to Gehenna. In the chapter on "General Peculiarities"
it will be pointed out that the Gehenna referred to by this Targum is the Messianic doom.

The major principles of the exegesis of the Targum can
be placed under four headings; namely, the allegorical, the
metaphorical, the complement and the lexical. The allegorical
shall be considered first.

The allegorical method was employed in the Agada and
by Philo, and to a larger extent by the Apostles and latter
Church Fathers.[8]   But it is to be noticed that the targumist

---

5)   Com. Am. 9:1;   Ze. 11:7-11, particularly v. 10.   On the other
hand, com. Ze. 6:5—the "four kingdoms" are not called by name.

6)   Com. Is. Ch. 9, 11, 12, 6-5;   Jer. 23:3-9;   Hos. 6:1-4;   14:15,
etc.

7)   Com. Is. 24:19-18;   25:4-5 ;   Ch. 32;   33:13;   Jer. 23:28;   Hab.
2:4;   3:2, etc.

8)   The two former need no illustration. With regard to the N. T.,
Jesus himself was addicted to it (Com. Mat. 21:42, Luk. 4:16-22).   With
regard to Heb. Ch. 8, Riehm (Lehrb. p. 204, ed 1867) remarks: "The
author leaves out of consideration the historical meaning of Old Testa-
ment passages."

confines the application of this method to passages which garb an implication. Whether or not he strikes the right point he is distinctly approaching it. He is making no strange and artificial combinations. In most cases his exposition falls in line with the Agadic interpretation.

The larger portions treated allegorically by the T. are Ez. 16, Hos. 1:2, 5, 6, 8; 3, 1-4. Ch. 16 in Ez. is turned by the T. into a reahearsal of the History of Israel: ". . . your habitation and your birth was in the land of the Canaanites, there I was revealed to your father Abraham between the pieces (Gen. 15:9-18) and I announced to him that you shall descend into Egypt, (and that) I (shall) deliver you with an uplifted arm, and on account of your ansectors I (will) expell from before you the Amorites and destroy the Hitites. And then your ancestors descended into Egypt, inhabitants in a land which is not theirs, enslaved and oppressed. . . The eye of Pharaoh did not pity you, to render unto you one generous act, to give you respite from your bondage, to have mercy on you, and he decreed concerning you ruinous decrees to throw your male children in the river to destroy you, while you were in Egypt. And the rememberance of the covenant of your ancestors came before me and I was revealed to deliver you, for it was divulged before me that you were oppressed in your bondage, and I said unto you by the blood of circumcision I will pity you, and I said unto you on account of the blood of the Passover (sacrifice) I will redeem you. And I was revealed unto Moses in the bush, for you, and I put off your sins and swore to deliver you as I swore to your ancestors, in order that you shall be a people serving before me. And I delivered you from the bondage of the Egyptians. And I lead you (forth) in freedom. And I clothed you with painted garments from the riches of your enemies (Exod. 14:21) and I sanctified priests from your midst to serve before me. . And I reformed you in the reform of the words of the Law written on two tablets of stone and (which) I gave them through Moses. And I gave in your midst the Ark of My covenant and the cloud of My Glory on you and an Angel sent from before Me leads at your head. And I gave My Tabernacle in your midst fitted out with gold . . . and you became very rich and very powerful and you prospered and ruled over all kingdoms."

Whether this exposition is right is open to question. The portion beginning with v. 7 may refer to the Kingdom of Solomon as well. But that it was allegorically framed is evident, and the T. only follows the current interpretation traceable in the Agada.[9] On the other hand, it should be noticed, the targumist asserts the dependence of his exposition on the text. On the whole, however, it runs like a Midrashic treatise. The phraseology is free in the use of parenthetical phrases and synonyms.[10] The textual form is paid little heed.[11]

Hosea, 1:2-5, 8; 3:1-4, comprising the command of God and the action on the part of Hosea to take to himself "a wife of whoredom", are interpreted in the T. allegorically. Accordingly, the rendering is put in this way: "Go and prophesy on the inhabitants of the city of the idols who increase in sin (v. 2). And he went and prophesied to them that if they repent they will be pardoned, and if not they will fall like the falling of the leaves of a fig tree (גמר בת דבלים) and they increased and committed evil deeds (vv. 3, 6, 8) and their generation, exiled among the peoples, were not acceptable (רחימין) in their deeds. And God spoke to me again: Go and prophesy on Israel who resemble a woman who is beloved of her husband and betrays him (3:1). And I redeemed them on the fifteenth of Nisan, and I put the Shekel as atonement

---

9) The interpretation of the T. as a whole is in full agreement with the Agada. It is generally accepted that this passage refers to the deliverance from Egypt (com. Sota 11b). V. 6, which the targumist refers the repeated בדמיך חיי to the blood of circumcision and Passover, is so interpreted in Seder Eliahu r. 25 (p. 138 F.); Mechilta 21,5; Pesiqta r. 15 F. (Com. Note 46). On the other hand, the interpretation of v. 10 as referring to the booty of the drowned Pharaoh is applied by the Agada to v. 7 (Mechilta), while v. 10 is interpreted as referring to the priestly garments and to the Mishkan (com. Jalqut l. c.). To the latter the T. refers v. 13, while it agrees with the former. In the interpretation of v. 11 the T. is in accord with the Agadaist (ibid).

10) Com. particularly vv. 4, 7.

11) Com. vv. 4, 5, 6, 10.

for themselves and I said that they shall bring before Me the Omer of the offering from the produce of barley." (v. 3).[12]

The allegorization in this case is somewhat peculiar. The text requires the literal conception of the act which, in its fulfilment, carries both the situation and reality of the prediction. It was taken in the literal sense by the Agada.[13] That some agadist, however, would have it allegorically interpreted and that the T. is following his interpretation is fairly certain.[14] The reason, however, for the exposition can only be the horror the targumist must have felt at the supposition that the prophet would be told by God to take a harlot to wife. The absence of such a cause is probably the reason why Zech. 6:1-9 is rendered literally.

The Servant of God is by the T. identified with the Messiah, whose approaching appearance has been expected by his contemporaries. That being the case, the allegorization on the same lines of Is. 53 must follow as a self evident result. This had been the case with all those adhering to the allegorization of the Servant of God. But the targumist is strikingly

---

12) Com. Chull 92b: "And I bought her for me for fifteen pieces of silver", R. Jonathan said: . . for fifteen (means) this is the fifteen Nissan, when Israel was redeemed from Egypt." So Pesiqta 15. On the other hand, the latter part of the verse is interpreted differently (ibid).

13) Com. note 18. Com. Pesiqta on 3:3: תניא ר' חייא אומר : לא תזני לא תעשה פסל ; ולא תהיי לאיש לא יהיו לך אלהים אחרים.
Com. P'sachim 87a end. "The Holy One Blessed Be He said to Hosea: 'Thy children sinned', and he should have said: 'They are Thy chiuldren, the children of Thy favored ones, Abraham, Isaac, and Jacob, show Thy mercy to them'. Not only did he not say so, but said, 'exchange them for another people'. Said the Holy One, Blessed Be He: 'What shall I do to this aged one? I'll say to him: Go and take for yourself a harlot and have for you harlot children, and then I'll say to him, send her away from your presence; if he can send (her away), I also will send away Israel. For it is said: and the Lord said to Hosea, etc.'' The Agada goes on to tell that after two sons were born to him God intimated to him that it would be proper for him to divorce her. Upon which Hosea refused to comply and God then said to him: "If this be the case with your wife, being a harlot, and thy children being children of whoredom, and you know not whether they are yours or belong to others, how should it be with Israel," etc.

14) Com. Jalqut l. c.

singular. Assured that this prediction is about the Messiah,
the targumist reverses the simple meaning of the words, transforming the gloomy portraiture of the Messiah into an image
of magnificence and splendor, unlike the Agadist contemporaries,
who would rather play thoughtfully on the humbleness and
sufferings of the Messiah.[15] He was influenced by the great
national movements of his time, which assumed a Messianic
character. So, while he would, seemingly with this end in view,
change in 52:14 the p. only as if Israel and not the Messiah
is the object, he actually rewrites ch. 53, replacing it by one
bearing no resemblance to the original.

Instead of the Messiah being regarded as of no form, no
comeliness, of no beauty (v. 2), he becomes one of extra-
ordinary appearance, differing from the appearance of the
former Davidic Kings, his terror unlike that of the profane
king; for his countenance will be a holy countenance. Who-
ever will see him will gaze at him (v. 3). Describing how
he was despised, rejected and a man of sorrow, he makes it
refer to the kingdoms whose glories will be destroyed by the
Messiah. So, the rendering of the T. runs: "For our sins he
will supplicate and our transgressions will be pardoned on
account of him. We are considered stricken and oppressed
from before the Lord." Note the rendering of v. 5: "And
he will build the Temple, which was desecrated through our
sins, delivered to the enemies for our transgressions, and
through his teaching peace will abound for us, and by our
gathering of his words our sins will be forgiven to us." In
this spirit the rendering is carried on to the end of the chapter.

THE METAPHOR

Prophecy is clothed in the magnificent form of poetry.
It directs its thoughts in a superfluity of imagery. The over-
coming force with which the prophet perceived his vision and
the vehemence with which, "like a fire," it is impelled to come
forth, make the metaphor the instrumentality of prophetical

---

15) Com. San. 98a, Pesiqta Rabati 36.

speech. It is addressed in terms of nature and natural phenomena, leaving the emphatic to the layman to unveil and distinguish. The targumist made it a principle to render not the metaphor but what it represents, the event described and not the description. It is the purpose which is of chief import to him. In a way this is with him rather a principle of translation, as in most cases there can be no claim to exegetical examination.

The parabolic metaphor is the prophetic parable which resolves itself less in event than in metaphorical presentation. The T. instead of giving the literal rendering of such a parable renders its underpoetical parallel, thus stripping it of its parabolic nature.

Except for the substitution of the simple for the metaphorical, the T., as a rule, in these cases keeps closely to the text stylistically as well as grammatically and synthetically. Exceptions to this rule are Is. 5:1-3; 5-7. The substitute is the one made obvious by the text, with the exception, again, of the parable in Is. 5, where somewhat far-fetched substitutes are used. Otherwise the T. will introduce its equivalent by the short phrase דהוה דמא "which is equal", and insert, where such is required for better understanding, a complementary word or phrase.

A few verses of each case of the parabolic metaphor will sufficiently illustrate the application of this principle. This will best be accomplished by placing the rendering of the T. side by side with the original.

Ez. 19:3, 6

V. 3

T.	H.
And she brought up one of her children, he became a king, and he learned to kill, killing, men he killed.	And she brought up one of her whelps, he became a young lion, and he learned to catch the prey, he devoured men.

V. 6

T.	H.
And he went up and down among the kings, he became a king and he learned to kill, killing, men he killed.	And he went up and down among the lions, he became a young lion; and he learned to catch the prey; he devoured men.

Ez. 23:2, 5

V. 2

Son of man prophesy on two cities which are like two w o m e n who were the daughers of one mother.	Son of man, there were two women, the daughters of one mother.

V. 5

And Ohlah erred from my worship and she was wilful to err after her lovers, the Assyrians, her near ones.	And Ohlah played the harlot when she was mine, and she doted on her lovers, on the Assyrian warriors.

Ez. 31:3-15, however, is rendered by the T. in a more detached manner. This is due to the fact that while it constitutes a similitude it is framed as a comparative metaphor. Assyria is here likened to a cedar in Lebanon, around which turns the entire description. The T., translating it as a description of the greatness and strength of Assyria according to the implication, had to change the p. as well as the number. Otherwise it keeps the rendering in line with the original.

The poetical metaphor, forms of expression given in objects of nature, is treated in the same manner by the T., namely, the object represented by the description is rendered. In this case also closeness to the original is observed, while a circumscription of phraseology is predominantly maintained. But, as if it were a concession on the targumist's part to the poetical element in prophecy, the insertion, "it is equal", "like", is, with few exceptions, not employed in such cases. Examples of this sort are: Is. 2:13: "And upon all the cedars of Lebanon that are high and lifted up, and upon all the oaks of Bashan." The T. renders it: "And upon all the princes (רברביא) of the strong and powerful and upon all the tyrants (טורני) of the lands (מדינתא); or Is. 9:9: "The bricks are fallen, but we will build with hewn stones; the sycamores are cut down, but cedars will be put in their place." T.: "The chiefs were exiled but better ones we will appoint, property (נכסיא) was spoiled, and more excellent we will buy." Other examples of this sort are: Is. 10:18, 19; Ez. 9:4, 5; Hos. 7:9; Joel 2:25 etc. Finally, the targumist is not consistent in the selection of the substitute figures. (Com. רעים Jer. 2:8; Ze. 11:3 rendered by מלכיא , while in Ez. 34:2, 5, 7 etc., it is rendered by פרנסיא (עצים Ez. 24:5 and 24:10). The rendering of the T of the comparative metaphor, i. e., the metaphor employed expressly for comparison, rests on the same basis, but it is effected in a different way, namely, both the literal and the implied rendering of the metaphor in question is given. An illustration of this sort of rendering is Is. 28:2: "Behold, the Lord hath a mighty and strong one. As a storm of hail, a tempest of destruction. As a storm of mighty waters overflowing, that casteth down to the earth with violence," which the T. renders: "There is a mighty and powerful stroke coming from the Lord as a storm of hail, as a tempest, as a storm of mighty waters overflowing so will peoples come upon them and will exile them in another land for their sins." Other examples are Is. 8:6, 7; 17:6; Jer. 2:24. In this particular instance the T. instroduces the necessary complement which the poetical language implies.

In other cases the T. assumes a comparative metaphor and renders it accordingly, the literal is then put after the implied one and the comparative דכן or כ is inserted. Instances of this sort are numerous. Com. Ez. 2:6; Hos. 8:7; 10:71, 16; 12:2 etc.[16]

---

16) As to the scope of the application of the metaphorical princile it should be noticed that although applied in full measure of persistency, it still has a multitude of exceptions. These excetions occur particularly in those parts of the Prophets where the T. is predominantly

The symbolic expression is rendered in the T. in its simple sense, as the text would indicate. No comparative is employed. Instances of this sort are Is. 6:6; Ez. 2:8; 3:1, 2, 3. Some meta-phorical expressions are rendered allegorically by the T., in which the T. is following a Midrashic course. The rendering is free in every respect. An instructive example of this sort is Am. 4:14: "That maketh the morning darkness and treadeth upon the high places of the earth." Targum: "To set light to the pious like the light of the morning, which is setting, to bring darkness to the wicked, to break the wicked of the land." Other examples are Is. 42:11, 57:16; Am. 8:13.

A principle extensively applied in the T. is one that may be described as the exegetical complement. This, in the first place, was intended to fill the gaps created by the poetical contraction of the prophetical style. In some cases a complement is dictated by the sense of the passage. This will be fairly well demon-strated by the following passages:

Mal. 1:4: "Whereas Edom saith we are impoverished but we will return and build." The sense of this passage requires some linking word between "impoverished" and the rest, as being impoverished, it is impossible to build. In order to fill this gap, the T. renders it this way: "We are impoverished **now we are enriched** we will return," etc.

Jer. 17:4 ושמטתה ובך מנחלתך the shortcomings of this pas-sage need not be pointed out. (Com. Lxx and particularly P. on this v.). The T. supplies both ובך and מנחלתך with com-plements to fill the gap, rendering: "And to you I shall render a **punishment of judgment** until I **shall exile you from your in-heritance.**" Com. also Is. 10:15; Hos. 2:15; Ez. 7:13; 16:29; 38:14 etc. In other cases the passage is supplemented by the T. with a view to simplify it where such a step is considered necessary. Here are some examples: Ez. 20:29: "What is the high place whereunto ye go," which is supplemented in the T.: "whereunto ye go **to make yourself foolish**" (worshipping the idol). Hos. 2:1: "The number of the children of Israel

---

literal. Com. Jer. 51:13; Ez. 34:4; Joel 2:2, 3; 3-6; Am. 3:12, 15; 5:19; Mi. 4:7, and a few others.

shall be as the sand of the sea." The T. inserting a complement renders it: "Shall be **numerous** as the sand," etc. Other cases of this category are: Ez. 20:9; 33:24; 44:19; Hos. 2:11, 16; 8:1 etc. The T. again is inclined to provide the substantive for the pronoun in cases where it is not sufficiently obvious. Three passages from Ez. will serve the purpose of illustration. Ez. 1:4: "And out of the midst thereof." This pronoun the T. substitutes by the noun rendering: "And out of the midst **of the cloud and out of the midst of the whirlwind**" (both of which are mentioned in the v.). Ibid v. 13: "It went up and down" etc. The T. replaces the "it" by the fire. Ibid. 29:5: "Upon the field shall it (taking the 3rd p.) fall." Targum: "Thy corpse shall be thrown." (Com. also Ez. 45:8; Jer. 6:1.)[17]

Repetition of the same word or of identical words, considered as one of the principles governing the exegesis of Philo,[18] affords the targumist a cause for introducing an exegetical complement, thus transforming the single word into a clause. The obvious reason for this, it would appear, is the disregard of the targumist of the poetical chord of prophecy so persistently insisted upon by the T. in each exegetical turn. He was unable to resist the conviction, so effective with the Halaka and Agada, that each of the repeated words must possess independent significance and carry independent implication. However, he is not explaining it but complementing the repeated word, heading, as a rule, the clause. Here are a few illustrations: Is. 6:3: "Holy, holy, holy is the Lord of Hosts." Targum: "Holy (is He) in the high lofty heavens, the house of His Shekina; holy on the earth the work of His strength; holy in the world of worlds." Jer. 7:4: "The temple of the Lord, the temple of the Lord, the temple of the Lord are these." Targum: "Before the temple

---

17) An interesting case presents Is. 28:10. The complement is supplied in an ingenious way to obviate the difficulty in this verse. The rendering runs: "For they were commanded to observe the Law and they were commanded (to do) they wanted not to do, and prophets prophesied to them . . . and the words of the prophets they did not accept." Observe: לצו is treated thus לא צו and so with לקו.

18) Com. Siegfried, Philo, etc., p. 168, put by Briggs (Biblical Study, p. 306) in group II.

of the Lord ye worship, before the temple of the Lord ye sacrifice, before the temple of the Lord you bow three times through
the year." Com. Is. 2:19; Jer. 22:29; Ez. 16:23; 21:14;
36:3. As to identical words, com. Is. 1:2; 33:22; 43:12.

Finally it should be noticed, that though the principle pointed
out in the foregoing instances is Midrashic in nature, the complement is simple, concise, and in considerable measure keeping
within the boundaries of the text.

On one plane with the metaphorical principle rests the
lexical. This principle affects singular words or expressions
which, though not metaphorical, bear a poetical stamp, and in
reality convey more or less the idea of the meaning than the
meaning itself. Such words or expressions, instead of rendering
them according to their surface meaning, the targumist takes
them by their underlying value as suggested by the text. Instances of single verbal words: Ez. 12:13: "And I shall bring
him in Babel." Targum: "I shall exile him" etc. So also v. 16;
36:20 etc. ibid. 23:10: "they took", Targum: "they captured";
Hos. 4:3: "Therefore doth the land mourn." Targum: "Therefore shall the land be laid waste". Ibid. 13:5: "I did know thee
in the wilderness" — "I supplied your needs in the wilderness."
Instances of nouns: "And I will appoint over them four families"
— "four calamitious afflictions." In Mi. 2:3: "On this family"
— "generation; Ez. 24:8: "I gave her blood" — "I revealeth
their transgressions"; ibid. 21:37: "they blood" etc. — "the
sin of your murder." Ez. 34:2: "Prophesy on the shepherds of
Israel" — "on the leaders (פרנסיא) of Israel." Instances of expressions: "And they shall do with thee in hatred" — "and
shall revenge from thee" etc. Ez. 16:16: "not coming and not
being (so)" — "not as required nor proper; Ez. 13:17 etc.:
"put thy face" — "accept prophecy". Examples of all categories
are numerous.

In drawing a comparison between this Targum and
Onk., as well as other translations with respect to the exegetical principles, it will appear that Onk. pursues the same principles. This point was well elucidated by Luzzato in Oheb.
Ger. 31. As regards the other translations, some exceptions must
be made. The allegorical principle as well as the metaphirocal,

as applied by the Targum, are to be found neither in the Lxx nor in P. On the other hand, the principle of the exegetical complement is followed by the Lxx in Pentateuch [19] and in a lesser degree also by the P. Illustrations are: Gen. 25:22: "And she said: 'If it be so, wherefore am I'," which the Lxx render: εἰ οὕτως μοι μέλλει γίνεσθαι etc. Gen. 40:16: "in my dream" κἀγὼ ὕδεν ἐνύπνιον
In the Prophets this is evident to a lesser degree. It found, however, application in this part also. Com. Zech. 14:7: "And there shall be one day which shall be known" etc. Lxx ἔσθαι μίαν ἡ ἡμέραν καὶ ἡμέρα ἐκείνη γενεστὴ etc. So. P. Com. also P. Hos. 2:11 (8).

The lexical principle also was pursued to some extent by the Lxx, and in a lesser degree by P. Com. Gen. 13:2: "And Abram was very heavy." Ἀβρὰμ σὲ ἐν πλούσιος So P. 15:2 עֲרִירִי ἀτέκνος . So. P. (Onk. agreenig in both instances). But com. Lxx T. Jer. 22:30, 49:3: ראשית אני — ἀρχὴ τέκνων (P. lit. Onk. Alleg.) v. 10: — שבט ἄρχων (P. lit. Onk. Alleg.) etc. Is. 8:4 במכני Lxx ἐν τῇ ἐμῇ πόλει

Apart from these major principles there is an element of commentary in the exegesis of Jonathan. At the first glance it be- comes clear, that the tendency of this commentary is merely to explain away the harassing difficulty. No heed is exhibited to the text, no effort to fit it into the phraseology of the respective passages. So Mi. 2:8: ...לאויב עמי ואתמול — "My people is delivered because of their sins; because of them existing peoples will inherit them." Compare also Is. 10:32, 32:19, 33:6; Jer. 4:9; Hos. 10:11; Mi. 2:11; Hab. 3:2; Mal. 1:11. But while this sort of commentary is somewhat of the nature of a homily, there is another phase of the exegesis resting on definite principles. The T. usually changes the interrogative into the categorical. This happens particularly with such interrogative phrases which, in the first place, imply a definite answer, and, in the second place, the implied answer is not given in any form. It should be observed that the Lxx in Pentateuch also employs such a

19) A most elucidative treatment on these points in the Lxx is found in Z. Frankel's "Über den Einfluss" etc. See particularly pp. 4, 9, 73.

device.[20]   The following are examples: Is. 66:9: "Shall I bring to birth and cause to bring forth? Shall I that cause to bring shut the whomb?" Targum: "I (am) the God who created the world from the beginning. I created all men and I spread among the people. I shall gather thy exile." Jer. 18:14: "Doth the snow of the Lebanon fail from the rock of the field? Or are the strange cold flowing waters plucked up?" Targum: "Behold, as it is impossible that the water snow running down the fields of Lebanon shall cease, so will not cease rain coming down and welling water from the source." Compare also Ob. 1:12, 15. Another interesting characteristic device of the commentary is the turning of one part of the verse into a complement of the other part. Some examples will well illustrate this point. Is. 5:20: "Woe unto them that call evil good and good evil, that change darkness into light and light into darkness, that change bitter into sweet and sweet into bitter." Targum: "Woe who say to the wicked ye are good, and unto the humble be said you are wicked, behold when light will come to the just will be dark for the wicked, and sweet will be the words of my Torah to those observing them, and bitterness will come to the wicked." Am. 5:12: "Ye that afflict the just, that take a ransom." Targum: "Ye that afflict that just **in order** to take mamon of falsehood." Compare also Ze. 11:8.[21]

---

20)   Com. Gen. 18:7; 27:36. Com. Z. Frankel, Vorstudien, p. 171. Über den Einfluss, 76.

21)   The T. turns a comparative phrase into a resultant, treating אם as כן So Jerem. 22:28. Here the T. follows another principle, namely, turning one phrase of the v. into a comparative to the preceding one. Com. Is. 8:2, in which case an Agadic interpretation is involved (Mak. 24a); 42:2.

II.

The interpretative rendering of single words or phrases
is of a positive value. The interpretation is characteristic of
the early Palestinian exegesis. With little exception, they are
found in the Agada.

Joshua 7:1 וימעלו בני ישראל מעל Targum ושקרו בני ישראל
So Sifri Num. 7: ומעלה בו מעל (במדבר ה, יב) אין מעילה אלא שקר.
בכל מקום אלא שיקור... ואומר וימעלו בני ישראל מעל בחרם.
Onkelos l. c. and v. 6 has a similar rendering.

Joshua 10:13 (also 2S 1:18) ספר הישר Targum ספרא
דאורייתא. Com. Aboda Zara 25b. Also Y. Sota 1, 18.

מאי ספר הישר א"ר חייא בר אבא זה ספר אברהם יצחק ויעקב.
ר" אמר זה ספר משנה תורה דכתיב ביה (דברים ו) ועשית הישר והטוב.

Judges 5:10 רכבי אתנות צחרות Targum עסקיהון מבטלין דהוו
רכיבין על אתנן... ומהלכין בכל תחום ארעא דישראל ומתחברין למתב
על דינא...
So Erubin 54b רוכבי אתנות אלו תלמידי חכמים שמהלכין מעיר לעיר
וממדינה למדינה ללמד תורה.

ib. 5:31 ואהביו כצאת השמש בגבורתו Targum ורחמוהי יהון
בימי השמש. Com. Sifri Deut. 145 עתידין לאזהרא כזיהור יקריה
על הארין שיהיו פניהם של צדיקים כיום, וכן הוא אומר ואוהביו כצאת
השמש.

1 Sam. 1:1 מן הרמתים צופים Targum מתלמידי נבאיא. So
Meg. 14a. מן הרמתים צופים אחד ממאתים צופים שנתנבאו להם לישראל.
The Targum assumed הרמתים to be in const. state while צופים
as a descriptive noun as did P. Com. Lxx.
So is the Targum to 1S 9:15 בארץ צוף — בארעא דבה נביא דיי.

ib. אפרתי Targum אפרים דבית בטורא בקודשיא חולק.
siders Eli to have belonged to the Levites (1 Chronicles 6:18).
(So R. Jochanan Jalqut l. c.). The בני קהת were given a portion on the Mountain of Ephraim (Josh. 21:21). The Targum
in other cases (Judg. 12:5, 1K 11:26) merely transcribes it.
Com., however, Berachoth 31b.

1S 6:19 ויך בעם שבעים איש חמשים אלף איש Targum וקטיל
וקטיל בסבי עמא שבעין גברא ובקהלא חמשין אלפין גברא. Thus the dis-
crepancy in the number is eliminated. This interpretation agrees
with Y. San. 2, 4 ויך בעם שבעים איש ר' חנינה ור' מנא, וחד אמר

(pp. 58, 59,) סדר אליהו ר. and זו סנהדרין, וחמשים אלף מעם הארין
. Friedmann), לפיכך נפל מישראל חמשים אלף וסנהדרי גדולה עמהם

ib. 12:11 וית שמשון Targum וישלח ה' את ירובעל ואת כדן .
So Y. Rosh Hashana 2, 8; Babli 25a. Com. P.

ib. 13:1 כבר שנה דלית ביה חוביןTargum בן שנה שאול במלכו
אמר רב הונא כבן שנה שלא Y. Bikkurim 3, 3. בן שאול כד מלך
. Joma 22b אלא שנמחלו כל עוונותיו כתינוק בן שנה . טעם טעם חטא

ib. 15:17 בדם זכות שבטא Targum ראש שבטי ישראל אתה
Com. Sota 36b on רבנימין אבוך גרמא לך די בעו למעבר בימא
Ps. 68:28 היה ר' מאיר אומר בשעה שעמדו ישראל על הים היו השבטים
נוצחין זה את זה זה אומר אני ארד תחלה וזה אומר אני ארד תחלה
קפץ שבטו של בנימין וירד לים.
Also Tanchuma ויגש 8 on the same verse.

Com. וית נודא . Targum ואת כפיר העזים ib 19:13, 16
Schochar Tob as cited in the Jalqut l. c. והוא מוצא את התרפים
. Com. Kimchi l. c. בתוכה ואת העביט של עזים

So Ze- ib 19:18, 19 בבית אולפנא Targum וישבו בניות
bachim 54b אמר רבה וכי מה ענין אצל רמה ? אלא שהיו יושבין
ברמה עוסקין בנויו של עולם.

ib. 23:18 וימת ביום ההוא שמנים וחמשה איש נשא אפוד בד
Targum וקטל ביומא ההוא תמנן וחמשא גברין דכשרין למלבש אפוד
דבוץ . This interpretation of the expression implying that all
of them were high priests is followed in Y. San. 10, 2, Gem.
ויסב דואג האדומי... לא כן תני ר' חייה אין ממנין שני כהנים גדולים
. כאחת אלא מלמד שהיו כולם ראויים להיות כהנים גדולים

The T. 2S 1:19 אתעתדתון ישראלTargum הצבי ישראל
identified it with the root, יצב Com. Is. 21:5 Ps. Jon. Deut.
29:9. Com. Schochar Tob 22, 19:
אלהים נצב בעדת אל (תהלים פ"ב, א) ר' חני בשם ר' יצחק אלהים
עומד אין כתיב כאן אלא אלהים נצב צב איטימוס כמו דאת אמר (שמות
ל"ג, כ"א) ונצבת על הצור.
Both Onkelos and Ps. Jonathan render ונצבת by עתד·

Com. ib. 5:6 חטאיא וחביא Targum העורים והפסחים
שנואי נפש דוד שהיה דוד שונא עובדי ע"ז : פרקי דר' אלעזר 36

ib. 5:24 ויהי בשמעך את קול צערה הבכאים Targum
. Com. Shochar tob 27, 2 ויהי במישמעך ית קל צוחתא בריישי אילניא

אין לך רשות לפשוט יד בהן אפילו אם היו קרבין אצלך עד שתראה
ראשי האילנות מנענעין שנאמר ויהי בשמעך את קול צעדה בראשי
הבכאים and with minor alterations in Pesiqta Rabati 8.

דחליץ ומתגלי Targum כהגלות נגלות אחד הרקים ib. 6:20
The Targum interprets רקים empty, naked. Com. Jalqut l. c.
אמרה לו משפחת של בית אבא היתה נאה מטך, חלילה להם שנראה
מימיהן פסת יד ופסת רגל ועקב מגולה.
מהו אחד הריקים, אמרו עליו Com. Y. Sukka 5, 14; San. 2, 4
על בית שאול שלא נראה מהם לא עקב ולא אגודל מימיהם.

Targum ויך אלחנן בן יערי את גלית הגתי ib. 21:19
ויך אלחנן בן יערי אורגים זה דוד So Jalqut l. c. וקטל דוד בן ישי
בן ישי שחננו אל; בן יערי שהיה גדול כיער.

דאתנבי לסוף Targum ואלה דברי דוד האחרונים ib. 23:1
כך ישראל כשיבא Com. Shochar Tob 18, 5 עלמא לימי דנחמתא
משיח במהרה בימינו אומרים שירה.

וכשמשא דעתיד Targum וכאור בוקר יזרח שמש ib. 23:4
לאנהרא כזהיר יקריה על חד תלת מאה ארבעין ותלתא כניהור שבעת
כוכביא שבעתא ימיא. The T. was apparently influenced in
that by Is. 30:26 with minor changes. The Midrash also interprets it in a Messianic sense. Com. Midrash Shmuel 29, end:
אין אנו יודעים מהו וכאור בקר אלא כשיאיר הקב"ה בקר של משיח
וכאור בקר בעולם הזה כען; and in Pesachim 2a: תזריח השמש
זריחת שמש לצדיקים לעולם הבא. Com. R. Channel l. c.

ואיש יגע בהם ימלא ברזל ועץ חנית ובאש שרף ישרפו ib. 23:7
ואף על אנש דמשרי למיקרב בחובין אזלין ותקפין Targum בשבת
עלוהי עד דחפין ליה בלבוש פרזלא דלא יכלין במעי טורנין ורומחין
בכן לית פורענותיהון ביד אנש אלהין באשתא עתידין לאתוקדא יתוקרון
באתגלאה בית דינא רבא למתב על כורסיא דין למדן ית עלמא.
In a like manner runs the interpretation in סדר אליהו רבה 3,:
אבל פושעים של ישראל אינם כן אלא בקטנותם רכים ובזקנותם קשים
ומה שכרן? שמעלין ושורפין אותם בבית המקדש הגדול שלו שנאמר
ובליעל כקץ ואומר באש ישרפון בשבת.

אלין שמהת גבריא דהוי Targum אלה שמות הגבורים ib. 23:8
עם דוד גברא ריש משריתא על כורסי דינא. The interpretation of
גבורים as representing rather the learned who pronounce judgment, and not the warriors, is the favorite one in the Agada.
Com. Moed Katan 16b, Y. Mak. 6, 7 and Pesiqta r. 11.

מעידן דמתנכים Targum מהבקר ועד עת מועד ib. 24:15
מאי עת מועד אמר שמואל משעת שחיטת So Berakoth 62b תמידא.
התמיד עד ישעת זריקתו.   and in the name of R. Chiyya in
Pesiqta r. 11.

תרין אלפים ביתין ברטיבא. Targum אלפים בת יכיל IK 7:26
So Erubin 14b, Sifri Num. 42.
כתוב אחד אומר מחזיק בתים שלשת אלפים יכיל (דהי"ב ד, ה) וכתוב
אחד אומר אלפים בת יכיל ביצד יתקיימו שני כתובים הללו — אלפים
בלח שהם שלשת אלפים ביבש.

ib. 37 בירח זיו Targum זיו נצניא Com. Rosh Hashana
11a, Y. Rosh Hashana 2, 8 ההוא משום ? הכתיב נמי בחדש זיו
ראית ביה זיוא ואילניא .

בירחא דעתיקיא דקרן ליהTargum בירח האיתנים ib. 8:2
ירחא קדמאה ובען הוא ירחא שביעאה . In the Talmud (Rosh
Hashana 11a) R. Eliezer would interpret it to refer to the
"Aboth". The T. is based on this interpretation. At the
same time it intends to account for the change of the order
of the months following Josephus (Ant. 1, 3, 3) that it was
Moses who appointed that Nisan should be the first month
for their festivals. Com. PS Jonathan Exod. 12:2.

ib. 16:34 בית האלי Targum בית מימי So P. Com. San.
113a.

2K 2:3 תלמידי נבייא Targum ויצאו בני הנבאים . (So ib.
5, 7, 15; 4:1, 38; 6:1). Com. Sifri Deut. 131: ואומר ויצאו בני
הנביאים וכי בני הנביאים היו והלא תלמידיהם היו אלא מיכן לתלמידים
שהם קרוים בנים .

ib. 12 אבי אבי Targum רבי רבי . Com. Sifri l. c. וכשם
שהתלמידים קרוים בנים כך הרב קרוי אב, שנאמר ואלישע ראה והוא
מצעק אבי אבי ; Moed Katan 26a, where this Targum is quoted.

IS 1:23 דדף שלמונים Targum אומרין גבר לחבריה עביד לי
ודודף שלמונים: איכה Com. Pesiqta טבא בדיני ואשלם לך בדינך.
שלם ואשלם לך.

ib. 3:4 ותעלולים Targum וחלשתא. Probably according
to Chaggiga 14a אמר רב אחא בר יעקב אלו תעלי בני תעלי .

IS 4:3 כל דכתיב לחיי Targum כל הכתוב לחיים בירושלם
עלמא יחזי בנחמת ירושלים. This interpretation in a Messianic
sense agrees with San. 92b.

ib. 5:1 אשירה נא לידידי שירת דודי לכרמו כרם היה לידידי
אמר נביא אשכחיה כען לישראל דמתיל לכרמא Targum בקרן בן שמן
עשר קרנות Com. Lamentation r. 2, 3 זרעיה דאברהם רחמי.
and Menachoth 53a הן קרנו של אברהם שנאמר כרם היה לידידי.
ib. 2 So Y. Sukka 4, 16 . ואף מרבחי Targum ונם יקב חצב בו
Com. מנדל זה ההיכל יקב זה המזבח ונם יקב חצב בו אלו שיתין.
Sukka 49a שורק זה המקדש ויבן מנדל בתוכו זה מזבח ונם יקב חצב
בו אלו שיתין.

ib. 10 ארי בחובא דלא יהבו Targum כי עשרת צמרי כרם
בעון שאין מוציאין — ,Com. Pesiqta D'rav Kahana מעשריא.
מעשרותיהן בת עשר מידות של כרם עשר.

ib. 17 כמא דאמיד עליהון Targum ורעו כבשים בדברם
(from root דבר). Com. Pesachim 68a ר"א ,ורעו כבשים בדברם
מנשיא בר ירמיה אמר רב כמדובר בם.

ib. 18 וי דמשכן למחטי צבחד נגדין Targum הוי מושכי העון
Com. Suk. 52b, San. 99a חובין בחבלי למא אזלן וסגן עד דתקיפין.
א' רבי אסי יצר הרע בתחלה דומה לחוט של בוכיא ולבסוף דומה
כעבות העגלה שנא' הוי.
Also R. Akiba, Gen' r. 22, 2; Sifri Num. 112.

ib. 6:1 (2 Chronicles בשתא דאתנגע Targum בשנת מות
26:20). So Exod. r. 1, end. Jalqut l. c. אלא שנצטרע ? וכי מת היה
ומצורע חשוב כמת. Com. Ps. Jonathan, Exod. 2:23.

ib. 2 Targum בתרין בשתים יכסה פניו ובשתים יכסה רגליו
מכסין אפוהי דלא חזי ובתרין מכסי גויתיה דלא מתחזי .
Com. Pirke d. Eliezer, 4:

— ובשתים יכסה רגליו — שלא יביטו פני השכינה, ובשתים יכסה פניו —
שלא יביט בפני השכינה .

ib. 8:2 Targum ואעידה ערים נאמנים את אוריה הכהן
ואסהיד קדמי סהידין מהימנין ית לוטיא דאמרית לאיתאה בנבואת אוריה
כהנא והא אתו אף כן כל נחמתא דאמרית לאיתאה בנבואת זכריה בן
יברכיהו אנא עתיד לאיתאה.
This is exactly the interpretation of R. Akiba Makkoth 24b:
שוב פעם אחת היו עולין לירושלים כיון שהגיעו להר הבית ראו שועל
שיצא מבית קדשי הקדשים התחילו הן בובין ור"ע מצחק אמר להן לכך
אני מצחק דכתיב ואעידה לי וכי מה ענין אוריה אצל זכריה אלא תלה
הכתוב נבואתו של זכריה בנבואתו של אוריה, באוריה כתוב לכן בגללכם
ציון תחרש, בזכריה כתוב עוד ישבו זקנים וזקנות ברחובות ירושלים.
עכשו שנתקימה נבואתו של אוריה כידוע שנבואתו של זכריה מתקיימת.

ib. 9:4 ‏בי כל סאון סאן ברעש‏ Targum. ‏ארי כל מסבהון ברשע‏.
The interpretation is based on the transposition of the two
last letters of ‏ברעש‏. On the reading of the T. rests also the say‑
ing of R. Meir, Tos. Sota 3: ‏היה רבי איר אומר מנין שבמדה שאדם‏
‏מודד מודדין לו תלמור לומר כי כל סאון סואן ברעש.‏ Otherwise
the inference is hardly explicable. Apparently, the T. identified
‏סאון‏ with ‏שאון‏ formed from the root ‏נשא.‏ This was apparently
the underlying reading of the rendering of the Lxx, while P. and
I presume, also, Sym. read the same way and rendered it
accordingly.

ib. 10:16 ‏ותחת כבדו יקר יקד כיקוד אש‏ Targum ‏ותחות מני‏
‏יקרהון מיקד ייקדון.‏ The Targum interprets the phrase in the
terms of the current Agada that, for the purpose of rendering
the mircale of the destruction of the army of Senacherib more
pronounced, God caused the bodies of his host to be burned
within the raiments which were left intact. Com. the Syriac
Apocalypse of Baruch 63, 8: "And at that time I burned their
bodies within but their raiment and arms I preserved outwardly,.
in order that still more wonderful deeds of the Mighty one
might appear, and thereby His name might be spoken of through‑
out the whole earth." It was, it would seem, a current Agada.
Com. Tanchuma, ‏נח,‏ 21: ‏ומנין ברשעים בשעה שעלה סנחריב לירושלים‏
‏וכל חיילותיו עמו נשרפו גופיהם ולא נשרפו בגדיהם.‏ Also Lekach
Tob, Noach 9, 23. Com. Shab. 113b (and Rashi l. c.), San. 94a
‏א"ר יוחנן תחת כבודו ולא כבודו ממש כי הא דר' יוחנן קרי ליה למאניה‏
‏מכבדותי.‏ Com. Tos. San. 52a. ‏אותם‏

ib. 13:12 ‏אוקיר אנוש מפז ואדם מכתם אופיר‏ Targum ‏אחבב‏
‏רחלי מדהבא ועבדי אוריתא.‏ Com. also 32:2. In all other cases
the rendering of these two words is literal. Here the translation
was influenced by the Messianic nature which the targumist
assumes for this prophecy. The T. takes ‏אדם‏ to imply the
observer of the law following R. Jeremiah (Sifra Lev. 18, 5):
‏היה ר' ירמיה אומר מנין אתה אומר אפילו נכרי ועושה את התורה‏
‏הרי הוא ככהן גדול תלמור לומר אשר יעשה אותם האדם וחי בהם.‏

ib. 13:21 ‏ושעירים ירקדו שם‏ Targum ‏ושידין‏   Com. Sifri,
Lev. r. 5, 1; ‏ואין שעיר אלא שד שנאמר ושעירים ירקדו שם‏ :218 Deut.
‏וילדים ירקדון כאילין שריא כמה דתימא ושעירים ירקדו שם.‏

ib. 17:11 ‏ביום נטעך תשגשגי‏ Targum ‏באתר דאתקרשתון‏

למהוי עם תמן קלקלתון עובדיכון. The targumist evidently took
תישגשגי as based on the noun סיג, dross (Isaiah 1:25). Com.
Lev. r. 18, 3. כמד"א ביום שנטעתי אתכם לי לעם עשיתם פסולת
סיגים כסף היו.

ib. 19:25 ברוך עמי מצרים ומעשה ידי אשור ונחלתי ישראל
Targum ברוך עמי דאפקית ממצרים דעל דחבו קדמי אגליתי יתהון
The targumist. לאתור וכדו דתבו מתקרן עמי ואחסנתי יישראל
would not accept the literal and obvious meaning of this
verse placing the Egyptians and Assyrians on one footing with
Israel. In his view, therefore, the whole verse refers to Israel.
So was the view, apparently for the same rason, of the Greek
and the Syriac rendering of the verse.

Eliminating the insertions, this interpretation is found
in Hebrew ברוך עמי מצרים סדר אליהו זוטא (p. 194 Friedmann)
— עם שיצאו ממצרים, ומעשה ידי אשור — אלו שגלו לאשור והם
נחלת ישראל.

ib. 21:1 מטל משריין דאתין ממדברא Targum משא מדבר ים
משא מדבר ים אם ים למה מדבר אלא — כמעט Similarly Cant. r.
אלו ארבע מלכיות...

ib. 21:11, 12 שמר מה מלילה שמר מה מליל אמר שמר אתא
נביא פרייט להון ית נביאתא אמר נביא אית Targum בקר וגם לילה
אמרו Com. Y. Taanith 1, 1. אגר לצדיקיא ואית פורענות לרשיעיא.
לישעיה רבינו ישעיה וכי מה יוצא לנו מתוך הלילה הזה, אמר להם לא
כשאתם סבירין אלא בקר לצדיקים ולילה לרשעים. Com. also Pesachim
2a on 2S 23:4.

ib. 22:1 מטל נבואתא על קרתא דיתבא Targum משא גיא חזיון
נבייא עלה דאתנביאו בחילתא. This agrees with R. Jochanan (Pesichta Lam. r. 24) ר' יוחנן פתח משא גיא חזון גיא שכל החוזים מתנבאים
עליה. While Beraitha Taanith 28b would interpret it to refer
to the Tepmle. Rashi, however, would place the Beraitha in harmony with the interpretation of R. Jochanan.

ib. 8 על זין בית גנזי מקדשא. Targum על נשק בית היער
The T. was evidently prompted to this interpretation by IK
10:17, where it is called בית יער הלבנון interpreting לבנון to mean
the Temple, as he rendered 37:24 (2K 19:23), which coincides
with the explanation in Joma 39b.
א"ר זוטרא בר טוביה למה נקרא שמו יער דכתיב בית יער הלבנון לומר
Similarly Num. r. 11, 5. לך מה יער מלבלב אף בית המקדש מלבלב..

Com. San. 25b   טלטלא דגברא Targum   טלטלה גבר 17 .b
טלטלה גבר אמר רב טלטולא דגברא קשה...

ib. 18   קלון בית אדוניך Targum לא דלא ולתמן יתובון בקלן על
תנא הוא בקש קלון לבית .Com. San. l. c נטרתא יקר בית רבוניך.
אדוניו ולפיכך נהפך בבודו לקלון.

ib. 23 ותקעתיו יתד   Targum. אמניה אמרכל מהימן.   The targumist is of the opinion that שבנא was only אמרכל which dignity was to be transferred to Eliakim. Accordingly, he renders
פרנסא די ממנא על ביתא. (v. 15) This is the view of R.
Jehuda (Lev. r. 5, 3),   לך בא אל הסוכן א"ר אלעזר כהן גדול היה,
צנף יצנפך   ר' יהודה ב"ר אומר אמרכל היה. The T., however, to
(v. 18) יערי מנך ית מצנפתא would point to the opposite view,
that Shebna was a High Priest. (Com. T. 28:1).   The T.
to v. 18 has all the appearance of a Midrashic T., a portion of
which was incorporated here.

ib. 27:5   או יחזק במעוזי Targum אם יתקפון בפתגמי אוריתי
Com. San. 99b   א"ר אלכסנדרי כל העוסק בתורה לשמה משים שלום
בפמליה של מעלה ובפמליה של מטה שנאמר או יחזק במעוזי.

ib. 27:8   בסאסאה בשלחה תריבנה Targum בסאתה דהויתא
מנין שבגמרה שארם מודר בה מורדין לו שנאמר בסאסאה. So Sota 8b, San. 100a תניא היה רבי מאיר אומר כאיל בה יכילון לך

ib. 28:7   פקו פלילה Targum.   טעו דינהא.   So Meg. 15b,
San. 111b.   ואין פלילה אלא דיינים שנאמר ונתן בפלילים.

ib. 10   כי צו לצו קו לקו Targum אורייתא למעבד ארי אתפקדו
ומה דאתתפקדו לא צביאו למעבד סברו דיתקיים להון פולחן טעותא ולא
(p. 19, סדר אליהו רבה .Com. סברו לפולחן בית מקדשו (קו לקו)
Friedman) אתם, אי אתם כן אלא ששמין אתם טחי תפל מלעיבין אתם
על דברי כאילו אין בהם ממש ועושים אתם אותן צואה שאינה צואה קואה
שאינה קואה קואה צויתי אתכם בצאתכם ממצרים, צויתי אתכם בספר תוכחות
קויתי אתכם ארבע מאות ושמונים עד שלא נבנה הבית, חזרתי וקויתי
אתכם ארבע מאות ועשר שנים משנבנה הבית שנאמר כי צו לצו קו לקו.

ib. 29:1   הוי אריאל אריאל Targum מרבחא מדבחא   According
to Midoth 4, 7 it is the היכל Pesichta Lam. r. 26. But com.
Sebachim 53a, 59b, according to Rab.

ib. 17; 32:15   והכרמל ליער יחשב Targum קרוין סגיאין יתיב
Com. Caro   והכרמל ליער יחשב לחורשי דבי אינש   Com. Gen. r. 24, 1
l. c. and Rashi.

דרי תתובון לאורייתא Targum בשובה ונחת תושעון 30:15 .ib
תנוחון ותתפרקון. The Targum interprets בשובה to mean repentance and rendering the following as a resultant phrase. It agrees
with R. Eliezer, Y. Taanith 2, 8; San. 37b.
תניא אידך רבי אליעזר אומר אם ישראל עושין תשובה נגאלין. א"ל
רבי אליעזר כבר נאמר בשובה ונחת.

Targum ולא יכנף עוד מוריך והיו עיניך רואות את מוריך 20 .ib
ולא יסלק עוד שכינתיה מבית מקדשא ויהוון עיניך חזין ית שכינתיה
רב אחא בר חנינא אומר אף אין הפרגוד Com. Sota 49a בבית מקדשא.
ננעל לפניו שנאמר ולא יכנף עוד מוריך ר' אבהו אומר משביעין אותו
מוריך את רואות עיניך והיו שנאמר השכינה מזיו . Both, it would
appear, depend upon the interpretation of the Targum which
interprets מוריך to mean the Shekina, introducing the Temple
as a necessary complement.

תפתה 31:9 .ib Targum גהינם So Erubin 19a; Pesachim
54a; Seder Eliahu r. 29 (p. 150 Friedman).

ותנור בעיר ליה דראשא Targum ותנור לו בירושלים .ib
ר' ינאי ור"ש Com. Erubin l. c.; Gen. r. 6, 4 לדעברו על מימריה.
תרויהו אמרין אין גיהנם אלא יום שמהלט את הרשעים מה טעם הנה
(' ,'ג מלאכי) כתנור בוער בא יום . Mek. יתרו 9 : זה תנור והנה
גיהנם, שנאמר ותנור לו בירושלם.

כל דהוו מתאנחין מן קדם Targum כל אנחתה השבעתי 2 .ib
כל אנחתה השבתי כל אנחתה של בבל. So Cant. r. l. c. מלכא דבבל.

כמשכנא דלא מתפרק Targum אהל בל יצען 33:20 .ib
So Cant. r.
תני ר' אליעזר בן יעקב אהל בל יצען בל יצא ובל ינוע — כאהלי.

לא יתאמר עוד Targûm לא יקראו עוד לנבל נדיב 32:5 .ib
דרש רבי יהודה בר מערבא ואיתימא Com. Sota 41b לרשיעיא צדיקיא.
רבי שמעון בן פזי מותר להחניף לרשעים בעולם הזה שנאמר לא יאמר
עוד לנבל נדיב.

Targum כי ארמן נטש משש פראים מרעה עדרים 14 .ib
Com. Lam. r. ארי בית מקדשא חרוב אתר דהוא בית חידו הוה מבז
2, 5.

טוביכן צדיקא עבדתון Targum אשריכם זרעי על כל מים 20 .ib
Com. Baba Kama לכון עוברין טבן דאתון רמן לדזדעין על שקיא.
אמר ר' יוחנן משום רשב"י מאי דכתיב אשריכם, 17b, Aboda Zara 5b
Seder Eliahu Zuta 15 (ed. F.) כל העוסק בתורה ונמילות חסדים

אשרי מי שישם את. עצמו כשור לעול וכחמור למשוא וכפרה חורשת בשדה
שנאמר אשריכם זרעי על כל מים...

ib. 33:17 Targum מלך ביפיו תחזינה עיניך ית יקר שכינת
עתיד הקב"ה מלך עלמיא. Com. Seder Eliahu r. 14 (p. 168 F.)
לישב בבית המדרש הגדול שלו וצדיקי עולם יושבים לפניו שנאמר מלך
ביפיו. Eliahu Zuta 1 (p. 171 F.) ומנין שהיא מעלה ומושיבה את
נותנה נגר בסא הכבוד ואומר מלך . .

ib. 40:8 Targum. מית רשעיא יבש חציר Com. Schochar
Tob 1, 20 (ed. Buber) and citation in Jalqut: אבא תנחום
אומר למה הצדיקים דומים בעולם הזה לטבלא המקובעת באבנים טובות
ומרגליות וקערת ירק בתוכה נטלה הטבלא ונשפך מה שבתוכה נראה מה
שבטבלא כך נבלעו הרשעים מן העולם נראו הצדיקים שנאמר יבש חציר.

ib. 40:10 Targum הנה שכרו אתו ופעלתו לפניו הא אגר עבדי
Com. Tanchuma Gen. מימריה עמיה דכל עובדיהון גלן קדמוהי.
וכך אמר ישעיה אבל לצדיקים הנה שכרו אתו. 12 (Noach)

ib. 29 Targum נתן ליעף כח דיהב לצדיקא דמשלהן לפתגמי
אוריתא חוכמא The T. was influenced by 50:4, of which this
is the rendering. So Seder Eliahu r. 17 (p. 84 F.) אבל מלך
מלכי המלכים אינו כן אלא יושב בכסא שלו ומפרנס את הצדיקים בחכמה
בריעה שנאמר נותן ליעף . . . .

ib. 40:31 Targum וקוי ה' יחליפו כח יעלו אבר כנשרים ודסברו
לפורקנא דיי יתבנשון מכיני גלותהון ויתחדתון לעולימתהון. The reference here is to the Messianic era. Sifri (Num. 40) explains
it to refer to the future world which, however, might be taken
in an identical sense. Com. San. 92b, Jalqut Machiri l. c.

ib. 41:2 Targum מי העיר ממזרח צדק יקראהו לרגלי איתי
בגלאי ממדינחא אברהם בחיר צדקיא . This and the following verses
appear to have been generally explained to refer to the story
of Abraham's struggle with the four Kings (Gen. 14).   So
Shabath 15a, San. 108b, Tanchuma l. c. 19:
מי העיר . . . אמר הקב"ה אברהם העיר את עולמי בצדקו.
Com. Gen. r. 42, 1; Exod. r. 15, 50; Seder Eliahu r. 6 (p. 28
Friedman).

ib. 42:11 Targum ירנו ישבו סלע ישבחון מיתיא בר נפיקין
אף אבות ואמהות . Com. Gen. r. 13, 2, Jalqut l. c. מבתא עלמיהון
בתחית המתים כתיב ירנו Deut. r. 7, 3 . שנאמר ירנו יישבי סלע
יישבי סלע .

בדיל לזכאותה ישראל Targum למען צדקו 21 .ib.
בחדיש השביעי, ואימתי 40: The T is followed by the Pesiqta
הקב"ה דן את העולם ומזכה אותם ? בר"ה, שהוא חפץ לזכות בריותיו.
וכן הוא אומר י' חפץ למען צדקו, שהוא חפץ להצדיק בריותיו.
ר' חנניא בן עקשיא אומר רצה הקב"ה לזכות את Mak. 23b, Mish.:
ישראל לפיכך הרבה להם תורה ומצות שנאמר י' חפץ למען צדקו.

ואתן אדם תחתיך Targum עממיא ומסרית So Me-   43:4 .ib
chilta 10 מסכתא דנזקין and Exod. r. 15, 3: לבך קבע להם שמחה
שהוא נפרע מאויביהם שנאמר ואתן אדם . . .

אנכי הגדתי והושעתי והשמעתי Targum חויתי אנא   12 .ib
לאברהם אביכון דעתיד למיתא אנא פרקית יתכון ממצרים כמא דקימית
Similarly . ליה בין בתריא ואנא אשמעית יתכון אולפן אוריתי מסיני
אנכי הגדתי במצרים . . . והשמעתי בסיני. Jalqut l. c.

זה יאמר לי' אני וזה יקרא בשם יעקב וזה יכתב ידו   44:5 .ib
דין יימר מדחליא די' אנא ודין יצלי בשום יעקב ודין יקריב Targum
קורבניה. The interpretation approaches the Midrashic explanation of the verse to refer to four estates of the righteous ones.
זה יאמר לי אני אלו צדיקים גמורים וזה 36 Aboth of R. Nathan
יקרא בשם יעקב אלו קטנים בני רשע, וזה יכתב ידו לד' אלו רשעים
שפירשו מדרכיהם וחזרו בהם ועשו תשובה, ובשם ישראל יכנה אלו גרי
(מסכתא דנזקין And in a different way in Mechilta אומות העולם.
28) : וכך אתה מוצא בארבע כתות שהן עונות ואומרות זה יאמר לי'
אני ואל יתערב בי חטא מסגרים — זה שכולו למקום ולא נתערב בו
חטא, וזה יקרא בשם יעקב — אלו נרי צדק, וזה יכתב . . . — אלו בעלי
תשובה, ובשם ישראל יכנה — אלו יראי שמים.
Seder Eliahu r. 18 (p. 105 F.) is following Aboth of R. Nathan
מיכן אמרו לארבע כתים נחלקו ישראל באותה שעה, זה יאמר — אלו
צדיקים גמורים, וזה יקרא — אלו קטנים בני הרשעים, וזה יכתב —
אלו רשעים. The T. seems to follow this interpretation, although
it is less outspoken with regard to the last three which, however, allow themselves to be implied. Com. Sifri Deut., 119.

ראמר על בבל Targum האמר לצולה 27 .ib Com. Y. Berakoth
4, 1; Zebachim 113a; Shab. 113a; Lam. r. Pesichta 23 (Buber)
אמר ר' יוחנן האומר לצולה חרבי זו בבל.

לאסגאה עלה בני אנשא Targum לשבת יצרה 45:18 .ib It is
so interpreted in the Talmud as implying the obligation of
human reproduction. Com. Jebamoth 62a; Gittin 41a, etc.

מארעא רחוקא Targum מארץ מרחק איש עצתי 46:11 .ib

ד"א ברצות י' דרכי איש, זה אברהם בני אברהם So Gen. r. 54, 1. שנקרא איש, דכתיב ביה מארץ מרחק איש עצתי.

אלהים שלחני להתנבאה ואנא Targum פתח לי אזן ib. 50:5 מהו אומר בסוף ? ה' אלהים פתח לי אוזן, So Pesiqta 33 לא סריבת. הוא פתח לי אוזן לשמע קולו כשאמר את מי אשלח.

ארי מן קדם בישתא Targum כי מפני הרעה נאסף הצדק ib.57:1 דעתירא למיתי. The belief is here expressed that the death of the righteous one is a signal of an approaching calamity to escape which he is taken away from life. This was a prevalent belief derived from the interpretation of this verse.   Com. Baba Kama 60a: כיון שניתן רשות למשחית . . . ולא עוד אלא שמתחיל מן הצדיקים תחלה. א"ל אביי טיבותא הי לגבייהו שנאמר כי מפני הרעה... צדיק נפטר מהעולם רעה באה לעולם שנאמר הצדיק... San. 113a But com. Enoch 81, 9.

שלמא יתעבד לצדיקיא Targum שלום שלום לרחוק ולקרוב ib. 19 דנטרו אוריתי מלקדמין ושלמא יתעבד לתבו דתבו לאוריתא. Com. גדול השלום שנתן לעושי תשובה שנאמר שלום שלום... Sifri Num. 42:

ונלי קדמוהו דלית גבר Targum וירא כי אין איש ib. 59:16 וא"ר יוחנן אין בן דוד בא אלא Com. San. 98b דליה עובדין טבין. בדור שכולו זכאי או בדור שכולו חייב, בדור שכולו חייב דכתיב וירא כי אין איש . . .

ארי לית בר מינך Targum ומעולם לא שמעו ולא האזינו ib. 64:3 משליויהם של רשעים Com. Eliahu r. 20 דאת עתיד למעבר לעבדך לצדיקיא בעולם הזה אתה למד מתן שכרן של צדיקים לעולם הבא, ואומר ומעולם לא שמעו ולא האזינו... Com. also Shab. 63a; Exod. r. 45 end; Esther r. 1.

כמא דאשתכח Targum כאשר ימצא התירוש באשכול ib. 65:8 נח זכאי בדרא דטופנא. So R. Simon, Gen. r. 29, 1.

ארי דחייב עולים Targum כי הנער בן מאה שנה ימות ib. 20 בר מאה שנין יהי מאית. Com. San. 91a and Pesachim 68a. The interpretation of the T., however, agrees with Gen. r. 26, 3.

ארי כיומי אלן חייא Targum כי כימי העץ ימי עמי ib. 22 וחייו מנין שנאמר כימי העץ. (18) Com. Tan. Gen. 2 יומי עמי. Similarly Gen. r. 12, 5; Num. r. 13, 4. Lxx has a similar interpretation. Com. T. PS. 1:3 כאילן חיי — בעץ שתול.

זכרתי לך חסד נעוריך אהבת כלולתיך Targum Jerem. 2:2 דכירנא לכון טבות יומי קדם, רחמת אהבתכון דהימני במימרי ואזלי

בתר תרין שליחי בתר משה ואהרן במרברא ארבעין שנין בלא זורין.
אחרים אומרין]... כראי היא האמנה : 3 בשלח Com. Mechilta
שהאמינו בי שאקרע להם את הים, שלא אמרו למשה היאך אנו יוצאים
למדבר ואין בידינו מחיה לדרך אלא האמינו והלכו אחרי משה, עליהם
מפורש בקבלה הלוך וקראת... And in a modified form in Seder
Eliahu r. 17 (p. 85).

Targum מרוע אמרו עמי רדנו לוא נבוא עור אליך Jerem. 2:31
ר"א מרוע Com. Tanchuma Num. 2 אטלטילנא לא נתוב עור לפולחנך.
אמרו, אמרו לו נתת לנו בית מקרש וסלקת שכינתך ממנו עור לא נבוא
עור אליך.]ֹ.

איֹלו את חביב Targum נלער אתה לי ראש הלבנון ib. 22:6
עמלק, 2 : Com. Mechilta . קרמי מבית מקרשא רדם בריש טוריא
בקיש לראות את בית המקדש והראו, שנאמר את הגלעד ואין גלער אלא
בית המקדש שנאמר גלער אתה לי.

Targum וימת חנניה הנביא בשנה ההיא בחרש השביעי ib. 28:17
Com. Y. ומית חנניה נביא שקרא בשתא ההיא ואתקבר בירחא שביעא.
וימת חנניה הנביא... שנה אחרת היתה, ואת אמרת בן 5, 11 San.
אלא מלמד שמת בערב ראש השנה וצוה את בניו ואת בני ביתו
להסתיר את הרבר, שיוציאוהו אחר ר"ה בשביל לעשות נבואתו
של ירמיה שקר. Com. also v. 16.

ומשלם חובי Targum ומשלם עון אבות אל חיק בניהם ib. 32:18
אבהתא לבניא כר משלמין למחטי בתריהון. Likewise all Targumim
to Exod. 34:7 making it clear that the suffering sons are subject
to punishment also on their own account. This explanation is
איני והכתיב פוקר עון אבות על בנים that assumed in Berakoth 7a
וכתיב ובנים לא ימותו על אבות ורמינן קראי אהררי ומשנינן לא קשיא,
הא כשאוחזין מעשה אבותיהם בידיהם, הא כשאין אוחזין. The reference is to San. 27b.

וישמע עברא רמלבא Targum וישמע עבד מלך הכושי ib. 38:7
כיוצא ברבר אתה אומר וישמע עבר Com. Moed Katan 16b צרקיה.
מלך הכושי וכי כושי שמו והלא צרקיה שמו. But Sifri Num. 99
(mentioned anonymously by Rashi) would interpret it to refer
to Baruch b. Neriah.

והיה בתלתין שנין לזמן Targum ויהי בשלשים שנה Ez. 1:1
ראשכח חלקיה כהנה רבא ספרא ראוריתא. This numerical interpretation is given in Seder Olam. Com. Jalqut l. c.

מהוי הוה פתנם נבואה מן קרם ... Targum ... היה היה ib. 3
בארעא רישראל תב חנינות ואתמלל עמיה במרינת ארע כסראי. So Mech.

וי"א נדבר עמו בארץ ונדבר עמו בחוצה לארץ : (פסחא בא פתיחתא)
שנאמר היה היה, היה שנדבר עמו בארץ, היה שנדבר עמו בחוצה לארץ.
Also Rab Chisda Moed Katan 25a.

קול מלוליהן Targum קול המולה כקול מחנה בעמדם 24 .ib
It seems to follow . כד מודין ומברכין ית רבונהון קימא מלך עלמיא
the homily in Gen. r. 65, 5: ומה הוא בעמדם בא עם רם, בשעה
שישראל אומרין שמע ישראל המלאכים שותקין ואח"כ תרפנה כנפיהם.
Its repetition in the v. 25 is interpreted by the T. in the same
way, the silence preceding the word of prophecy descending
upon the prophet.

וכתיב ביה Targum וכתוב אליה קינים והגה והי 2:10 .ib
דאם יעברון בית ישראל על אוריתא ישלטון בהון עממיא ואם יעברון
ית אוריתא יסוף מנהון אליא ודונא. Com. chapter General Peculiarities. However a similar evasive interpretation is found in
וכתוב עליה קינים קינים של רשעים, והגה של צדיקים, Sifri Num. 103
והי של רשעים.

ולא מבניהון ולא מבני Targum ולא מהמהם ולא נה 7:11 .ib
נבחר מפנינים Com. Gen. r. 31, 1, as interpreted rightly in בניהון

ולא עבדתון לכון עוברין טבין Targum לא עליתם 13:5 .ib
למבעי על בית ישראל. Com. Jalqut l. c.; Esther r. 6.

וקרשית מנבון בהניא Targum ואחבשך בשש 16:10 .ib .
ואחבשך בשש אילו שמינה בגדי כהונה של כהן גדול Com. Pesiqta
שהיה בהם שש. The targumist, however, would interpret
ואבסך מישי as referring to the High Priest.

בתיבין על תרי לוחי אבנים Targum צמידים 11 .ib .
ואתנה צמידים אילו שני לוחות הברית. So Pesiqta 33

ומלאך שליח מן קדמי Targum ועטרת תפארת בראשך 12 .ib
ועטרת תפארת בראשך זו : גן נעול Com. Cant. r. מדבר ברישיכון.
השכינה; Pesigta 33.

וי"ת בלהות Kimchi כדלא הוית Targum בלהות אתנך 26:21 .ib
שתי מלים — בל הות. It is, it would seem, an old Midrashic interpretation. So Tanchuma Gen. 19 (Buber) מהו בלהות אתנך
ואינך, אומות העולם לא היו ולא עתידין להיות שנאמר בלהות . . .
בלהות בל היות.

ברם לא אסתכלת Targum מלאכת תפיך ונקביך בך 28:13 .ib
מלאכת תפיך... So Baba Bathra 77a. בפגרך דאיתעביד חללין ונקבין
אמר רב יהודה אמר רב אמר לו הקב"ה לחרם מלך צור נסתכלתי
ובראתי נקבים נקבים באדם.

Com. Ps. Jon. and Frag. Deut. 32:18, which is the interpretation of R. Meir, Sifri Deut. 227.

ib. 45:11 לשאת מעשר החמר הבת Targum סכום תלת מאין
מנא הני Com. Menachoth 77a למסב בורא במכלתא רטיבא ביתא.
מילי אמר רב חסדא קרא האופה והבת תוכן אחד היה, מה הבת שלש
סאין, ובת נופא מנלן, אלא מהכא וחק השמן הבת. The T. to v. 14 is
literal. The specification here of the number of kors is because
it forms the source for the inference of the measure of the epha.

Hos. 2:1 ...והיה במקום אשר יאמר להם לא עמי אתם יאמר להם
ויהי באתרא דאתגליאו כיני עממיא כד עברו על אוריתא Targum
ואתאמר להון לא עמי אתון יתובון ויתרבון ויתאמר להון עמיה דאלהא
קימא. This interpretation agrees with Sifri Num. 131 כיוצא בזה
אתה אומר לא עמי ואומר מספר בני ישראל וכי מה ענין זה לזה משל
למלך שכעס על אשתו שלח אחר סופר לבוא ולכתוב לה גט עד שלא בא
הסופר נתרצה לאשתו אמר המלך אפשר שיצא סופר זה מכאן חלוק אלא
אומר לו בוא כתוב שאני כופל לה כתובתה, לכך נאמר כי אתם לא עמי
ואומר מספר בני ישראל כחול הים. And Pesiqta 11. R. Meir,
however (Kidushin 36a), would not draw such a distinction.

ib. 2 כי גדול יום יזרעאל Targum ארי רב יום כנישתהון
אמר ר' יוחנן גדול יום קבוץ גליות כיום שנבראו בו So Pesachim 88a
שמים וארץ שנאמר כי גדול יום יזרעאל.

ib. 7 הוביש הורתם Targum. בהיתו מלפיהון. The T. explains
הורתם as of the root ירה to teach. It was so taken by others.
Com. Deut. r. 2, 2: א"ר שמלאי כתיב כי זנתה אמם הובישה הורתם,
שהם (הדיינים) מביישים דבריהם בפני עם הארץ. And the version
in Jalqut l. c. אמר ר' שמלאי אמר הקב"ה הדיינים מביישים דברי
בפני עם הארץ לכך נאמר כי זנתה אמם...

ib. וושקויי Targum פרנוסי. Com. Ketuboth 65a וושקויי
דברים שהאשה משתוקקת עליהן ומאי נינהו תכשיטין.

ib. 4:7 כרבם כן חטאו לי Targum כמא דאסגיתי להון עללא.
Deut. r. 2, 2 ד"א כל שהרביתי להן עושר כן חטאו לי. In a similar
way Lxx.

ib. 6:2 יחיינו מיומים Targum יחיינא ליומי נחמתא דעתידין
למיתי ביום אחיות מיתיא. The Messianic interpretation of this
v. was a current one. Com. San. 97a; Rosh Hashana 31a. Com
also Seder Eliahu r. 6: יחיינו מיומים זה העולם הזה וימות המשיח
וביום השלישי יקימנו זה העולם הבא.

ואינון בדריא קדמאי. Targum והמה כאדם עברו ברית 6:7 .ib
והמה כאדם... זה אדם הראשון, 4: .Com. R. Abahu, Psichta Lam. r
הכנסתיו לגן עדן וצוויתיו ועבד על צווי, אף בניו הכנסתי אותם לא"י
וצוויתים ועברו.Com. also Gen. r. 19, 7.

ועל דלא אדכרו נסין Targum מלוש בצק עד חומצתו 7:4 .ib
(פסחא, Com. Mechilta וגבורן דאיתעבידו להן ביום מסקהון ממצרים.
בא, 13 : מניד שלשו את העיסה ולא הספיקו לחמצה עד שנגאלו,
וכן אתה מוצא לע"ל דכתיב כולם מנאפים מלוש.

כספהון ודהבהון דאסיקו להון Targum כספם וזהבם 8:4 .ib
א"ר עקיבה הכל קראו תגר על הכסף Com. Gen. r. 28, 7 ממצרים
והזהב שיצא עמהם ממצרים שנאמר בכספם וזהבם עשו להם עצבים.
Com. also Lam. r., Pesichta 23 (Buber), interpreting in the
same way Ez. 7:19.

לא אעשה חרון אפי בקרבך קדושי לא אבוא בעיר 11:9 .ib
לא אעביד תקוף רונזי ולא אחליף בקרוא אוחרי עוד ירושלם. Targum
מאותה שעה נשבע הקב"ה לעמו שלא ישגם Com. Eliahu Zuta 10
בעם אחר ולא ישכינם בעיר אחרת שנאמר לא אעשה חרון אפי...
So Eliahu r. 22.

אתקשיט. Targum הכון לקראת אלהיך Am. 4:12 So Shab.
10a (Com. Rashi). Also Berakoth 23a.

ובידי אנך 7:7 .ib דין. Targum אנך Com. Lev. r. 33, 2
כבעל חוב ושטרו בידו... ואומר אנך זה סנהדרי גדולה של ישראל.

טפי מנרתא אתקטיל מלכא יאשיהו. Targum הך הכפתר 9:1 .ib
הך הכפתר זה יאשיהו Com. Lev. r. 33, 2.

הלא כבנין רחמין Targum הלא כבני כשיים 7 .ib . Com. On.
Num. 12:1, Sifri 99, Moed Katan 16b וכי כושית היתה והלא מדיינית
היתה, אלא מה כושי משונה בעורו כך צפורה משונה בנויה... כיוצא בו
אתה אומר הלוא כבני כשיים, וכי כושים היו ? אלא מה כושי משונה
בעורו אף ישראל משונים במצוות יותר מכל אומות העולם . So Shochar
Tob 7, 18. But ib. 14: כישראל חוטאים להקב"ה הוא קורא אותם
כושיים .

וקם יונה Targum ויקם יונה לברח תרשישה מלפני י' Jona 1:3
למערק לימא מן קדם דאיתנבי בשמא דיי' . The targumist desired to
thus eliminate the difficulty to explain the flight of the Prophet.
וכי מלפני ה' הוא בורח והלא כבר : פסחא, פתיחתא Com. Mechilta
נאמר אנא אלך מרוחך... אלא אמר יונה אלך לחו"ל שאין השכינה
נגלית שם. The targumist, however, has struck a plain and genial
interpretation by putting a complement to מלפני.

THE EXEGESIS   109

Mi. 2:13 Targum עלה הפורץ לפניהם כד משיזבין יסגון
בקדמיתא ויסק מלך מדבר. This interpretation seems to have been
held by r. Simon b. Aba (Gen. r. 73, 3) ויפרץ האיש ר׳ שמעון
בר אבא אמר מלמד שנפרצה לו פרצה מעין רונמא של עולם הבא היך
מד"א עלה הפורץ.

Mica 4:5 Targum ארי כל כי כל העמים ילכו איש בשם אלהיו
Com. Shochar Tob 1, 20 עממיא יהכון לאבדון על די פלחו לטעותא.
ר׳ אלעזר המודעי, לעתיד לבא באין כל שרי אומות העולם ומסטרגין
על בני ישראל לפני הקב"ה ואומרים לפניו רבש"ע אלו עובדי ע"ז... הללו
יורדי לגיהנם והללו אין יורדין ? אמר להם אם בן תרד כל אומה ואומה
ואלהיה עמה לגיהנם... שנאמר כי כל העמים ילכו איש בשם אלהיו.
Cod. Reuch has יהכון instead of לאבדון.

ib. 7:1 Targum אין אשכול לאכל לית גבר רביה עובדין טבין.
This interpretation is implied in Mishna Sota 47a (Y. 9,10).

Hab. 3:9 Targum שבעות מטות שבעה דעם שבטיא.
Com. Gen. r. 47, 7 א"ר יצחק כתיב כל אלה שבטי ישראל י"ב אלו
בני גבורה וישמעאל אינו מעמיד י"ב אלא אותן נשיאין אבל אלו מטות
ומניין שהקב"ה נשבע במד"א שבעות מטות... Also Exod. r. 44 end.
Com. also Sifri Deut. 117. לשבטים שנאמר שבעות מטות...

ib. 14 Targum נקבת במטיו בזעת ימא בחוטריה דמשה. Com.
עשרה נסים נעשו לישראל על הים, נבקע הים 2: Mechilta, בשלח
ונעשה כמין ביפה שנאמר נקבת במטיו...

Zef. 2:5 Targum גוי כרתים עמא דחיבין לאשתיצאה.
Com. Cant. r. גוי יחחיב כרת, מישכוני.

Zef. 3:8 Targum ליום קומי לעד ליום אתגליותי למידן. So in
Pesiqta r. 34 שבועה היא לפני, שכל שחיבה למלכותי אני בעצמי מעיר
לעד to mean בו לטובה שנאמר ליום קומו לעד The Agadist also took
to witness, from the root עוד. Com. also Exod. r. 17 end
אבל לעתיד לבא הוא עומד ודן את עולמו בעמידה... ובתיב לכן חבו לי
ביום קומי לעד.

Zech. 3:3 Targum ויהושע היה לבש בגדים צואים ויהושע הוו
So San. 93a ליה בנין דנסבין לחון נשין דלא כשרן לכהנותא אמר רב
ויהושע היה לבוש בגדים צואים וכי דרכו של יהושע ללבוש בגדים צואים פפא שהיו בניו נושאין נשים שאינן הגונות לכהונא ולא מיחה בהן שנא׳
אלא מלמד שהיו בניו נושאין נשים שאינן הגונות לכהונא ולא מיחה בהן.

ib. 8 Targum כי אנשי מופת המה כי אנשי גברין כשרין למעבד
Exod. r. 9, 1 כי אנשי מופת המה, איזו הם אנשים שנעשה להון נסין.

להם מופת הוי אומר זה חנניה מישאל ועזריה א"ל ידענא דצדיקא את
אלא מ"ט אהניא בך פורתא נורא וחנניה מישאל ועזריה לא אהניא בהו
כלל...

ib. 9:1 ורמשק מנחתו Targum מארע בית למהוי תתוב ורמשק
שכנתיה. Com. Cant. r. צוארך : ומה אני מקיים ודמשק מנחתו עתירה
Sifri Deut. 116. ; ירושלים להיות מגעת עד רמישק...

ib. 11:12 וישקלו את שכרי שלשים כסף Targum ועבדו ית
ואיני יודע אם '5 באן Saying of R. Jochanan רעותו גברין מקצת.
וט"ו בא"י ... כשהוא אומר ואחאת שלשים כסף הוי אומר ל"ו צדיקים.
This rendering is at the foundation of this Agada as well as
that of R. Jehuda, who finds in it the implication of the thirty
righteous ones among the Gentiles who exist by their virtue.

ib. 12:12 משפחת בית נתן לבר ונשיהם לבר Targum זרעית
והלא דברים Com. Suk. 22a .בית נתן גבריהון לחוד ונשיהון לחוד
ק"ו לע"5 שעוסקין בהספר ואין יצר הרע שולט בם אמרה תורה נשים
לבד ואנשים לבד עכשיו . . .

Malachi 1:1 ביד מלאכי Targum ביד מלאכי דיתקרי שמיה
תניא ר"י בן So R. Jehoshua b. Korcha, Meg. 15a: עזרא ספרא.
קרחא אומר מלאכי זה עזרא.

ib. 11 ובכל מקום מקטר מגש לשמי ומנחה טהורה Targum
וכי בכל מקום . . . Com. Num. r. 13, 2 . . . וצלותכון כקורבן דכי קדמי.
מקריב קטורת ומנחה לשם הקב"ה אלא בכל מקום שישראל עומדים
ומתפללים תפלת מנחה עליה נאמר מנחה... מגש זו תפלת שחרית... מקטר
זו תפלת ערבית.

ib. 2:12 אשר יעשנה ער וענה מאהלי יעקב ומגיש מנחה Targum
ואם בהין הוא לא יהי ליה קריב קורבנא Com. San. 82a; Shab. 55b
יברת י'... אם ת"ח הוא לא יהיה לו עד בחכמים וענה בתלמידים, אם
כהן הוא לא יהיה לו בן מגיש מנחה.

GENERAL PECULIARITIES

The Targum Jonathan reflects many interesting peculiarities which arose primarily from the state of mind of the age which produced the Agada and the Apocryphal literature. The Targum was read in public worship, and the translator would have to take full account of the susceptibilities of the worshipper. On the other hand, in the homilytic portions ample expression is to be found of the believes, expectations and views of that generation.

The targumist made it a principle to d i f f e r e n t i a t e between the holy and the profane. Words which are equally applied to the holy and unholy are rendered by the targumist by distinct words to maintain the difference. The Masorites follow a similar way. So that when חי is followed by the name of God it is vocalized with a patach (1S 20:3, 2S 12:15 etc.). While followed by a profane it is vocalized with a zeire. Genesis 42:15. (Com. 1S 28:26 חי יי וחי נפשך). The same tendency was made evident in the vocalization of אדני and in such forms as in the compound אדני צדק (Joshua 10:13) and אדני בזק (Judges 1:5, 6, 7). The targumist carried the principle to an extreme application.[1]

אלהים is applied both to God and the idol; the T. draws the distinction between them rendering the profane אלהים —

---

[1] Com. Geiger אוצר נחמד p. 3. Such a distinction has its parallel in the Talmud. So it is said (Shabbath 32a): "For three transgressions are women dying. Others say because they call the ארנא—ארון הקודש (box); R. Ishmael b. Elozor says: 'For the transgression of two things are the amei ha'arazoth dying: for calling the ארון הקודש Arna and because the Beth Ha-K'neseth is called Beth Am." No doubt, despite the unanimity of the commentaries that Arna and Beth Am are derisive, and for this reason their application to holy subjects was condemned, they desired to separate the holy from the profane. It would appear that this was urged only as a sort of mannerism. For the Talmud does not follow this distinction; in many passages Arna is employed in the sense of ארון הקודש (Com. Berakoth 47b).

טעון Joshua 24:14 והסירו את האלהים — טעון — So v. 15
Judges 5:8 אלהים חדשים — טעון   2K 19:18; Is. 33:37, 37:19
טעותהון — ונתן את אלהיהם באש. So also Jer. 2:10, 11; 11:12;
Hab. 1:11 etc. In order to avoid any semblance of imputation
of divinity to idols, the T. treats the adjective אחרים following
the profane אלהים as a noun, and אלהים as a noun in const.
state, thus rendering טעות עממיא — אלהים אחרים   So Josh.
20:16, 24; Judg. 2:12, 17, 19; Is. 26:19; Jer. 13:10,
16:11; 19:4, 13; 22:9 etc. In the same way is rendered
אלהי הנכר Josh. 20:23, 24; Jer. 5:19 etc. Probably this expression
has influenced the rendering by the T. of אלהים אחרים. Compare
Mech. יתרו ,5 : ומה תלמוד לומד אל הים אחרים, אלא שאחרים
קוראים אותם אלוהות. Equally is בעלים rendered. So Jer. 2:23
טעות עממיא — אחרי הבעלים. In some cases it is rendered like
the detached profane אלהים. So Jer. 2:8 והנביאים נבאו בבעל —
13:1 ; לטעותא — לבעלים יזבחו   Hos. 11:2   בשום טעותא .
ויאשם בבעל — לטעותא . Otherwise בעל is rendered by בעלא
(Jer. 7:9; 9:13 etc.).

This scrupulosity of the T. is strikingly illustrated by his
treatment of this term applied to idolatrous divinity, which is
made by the context to inevitably express godly divinity. So
אם צרך אית ביה יתפרע ליה בעלא — אם אלהים הוא Judges 6:31
This rendering which, it would appear, was suggested by such
passages as Is. 44:10; Jer. 2:8 etc., he applies also to 2K 19:18;
Is. 37:19 והמה לא אלהים as well as to the passage in Hos. 8:10
דלית ביה צרך — ולא אלהים הוא, "the unuseful one"; also Ez.
28:2, 9, in all of which the divine sense of אלהים is obvious.
But the targumist is anxious to avoid even an innocent profanation of this sort. On the other hand, when this profane
אלהים is not employed in the sense of incrimination but as a
fact the rendering is דחלתא "fear" [2]. So for instance 2K 18:33;
34:35; Is. 36:18; 37:12 : איה אלהי חמת ..החצילו אלהי הגוים'
וארפד — דחלתא or Jerem. 2:28; 11:13 כמספר עריך היו אלהיך

---

[2] The Talmud also employs its Hebrew equivalent יראה
So San. 64a, 106a. Also Y. Kidushin 1; P'siqta of Rab Kohna p. 65.
On the other hand, דחלא is employed in the divine sense also. See
Proverbs 1, 7: ריש חוכמתא דחלתא: F. Deut. 32:13 וכברו בדחלא תקיפא
ארי שבקתון דחלא תקיפא — כי נטשתה עמך   and Is. 2:6 די פרק יתחון

So also Jona 1:5 רחלתיה — ויזעקו איש אל אלהיו . Here it was only meant to state the plain reality. Com. also Ez. 28:2, 9.

In the case of the first two instances the targumist has merely identified the profane אלהים with the special name given to idols in the Bible, namely אלילים and גלולים, both of which he renders by טעון with the exception of the latter, which פולחן is in the most cases added to טעון . Com. Is. 8:8, 18, 20; 19:1, 3; Ez. 14:3; 18:6 etc. In this tendency the T. Jonathan is followed by Onkelos and the other Targumim only. With one exception, namely אלהים אחרים in the Ten Commandments (Exod. 20:3; Deut. 5:7), in which case Onkelos would not side-track the meaning, rendering them by אלהן אחרן (Ps. Jon. following On.). In all other cases On. also renders the profane אלהים — טעון (Exod. 23:24; 34:15; Deut. 12:2) and goes even with Jon. to render טעות עממיא — אל אחר . Of the other early translations no such distinction is noticeable, neither in the Pentateuch nor in any other part of the Bible, except in two cases in Lxx. These are: Num. 25:2. Com. Frankel, Über d. Ein., 175.

Usually מזבח is rendered by the targumist by the Aramic parallel מדבחא . But this rendering is applied only to the holy, to God's altar. Whenever it refers to the profane, referring to the idol either in stative or implied sense, it is rendered by אגורא, the pile. Ez. 6:4 וגשמו מזבחותיהם — אגוריכון . Hos. 8:9 מזבחות לחטא — אגורין; Is. 17:8; 27:9; Jer. 11:13; 17:12; Ez. 6:4, 6 etc. Accordingly ויאמר לפני המזבח הזה ואת מזבחותיו... (Is. 36:7) the former is rendered by אגורא the latter by מדבחא

In this case also, the Lxx and P. are making no such distinction. The only exception is the Targum Onk. and the other Targumim. They draw the same distinction and employ the same terms. Com. T. Exod. 34:13; Deut. 12:3; 7:5 etc.[3]

---

3) So the rendering by Onkelos יאכלו על הגל (Genesis 31:46) אגורא . A striking analogy to this is found in Mandaic, where עבורא is usually used to denote the worship of a false cult (Noeldke, Zeit. für Assuriologie, v. 20, p. 131). This distinction, it would appear, was not known to the Jews in Egypt in the fifth century B. C. The temple or shrine or altar of the Jews in Yeb is called אגורא (Sayce Aram. Pap. E. 14 אלה אלהא זי יהוה זי אגורא ; J. 6 אלהא יהו זי אגורא:Sachau (Aram. Pap. 1, 2). However, in Pap. 3 instead of אגורא the term em-

A distinction of this kind is traceable also in the Talmud. There is no particular name in the Talmud for the profane altar. But it has, however, special appelations for objects connected with the altar, one of which has a derisive air. So a sacrifice to an idol is called תקרובת a present.[4] Com. Aboda Zara 32b, 48b; Chullin 13b, 24a. But while the Targum to the Pentateuch reserves תקרובתא for the profane offering, the holy offering being rendered by קרבנא, תקרבתא is the judicial term, applied to idolatrous sacrifice in the Talmud using however קורבן to denote present. Com. Nedarim 20a כקרבנות מלכים ; Ab. Zara 64b. So does also T. Jonathan.[5] Com. Hos. 12:2 ושמן למצרים T a r g u m וקרבנא, although Korban is joined by the Tetra-gramm (Menachoth 110a, Sifra Lev. 2). Sometimes the idolat-rous sacrifice is called זבחי מתים (according to PS 106:28) Aboth 3, 3; Aboda Zara 29b; 32b.

Instead of זבח the usual verb for sacrificing, the Talmud in several places uses the verb זבל to manure.[6] Aboda Zara 18b; Y. Berakoth 9, 1; Pesiqta r. 6.

---

ployed is בית מדבחא . I am tempted to assume that this was prompted by this very desire of differentiating the holy from the profane temple. Here, the writer is a Jew and the writing was intended for Jews, and therefore he would not use the profane name אגורא for the holy temple. The others are documents of an official nature intended for the con-sideration of a Persian official or court. The current name of a temple would be used in such a case. Sachau's assumption (ib. p. 29) that אגורא was somewhat the intimate appelation among the Jews of the synagogue (p. 12) is not impressive. On the other hand, it is interest-ing to note that the priest of the temple is called Kohan זי כהניא יהו אלהא (Pap. 11), while the idolatrous priest is called Komer כמריא זי חנוב (Pap. 1 and Sayce E. 15 מרדוך בר פלטו כמר לחנוב). However, there is not sufficient ground in this to justify the assumption that even then the Jews would observe a distinction to which later generations adhered. The writer might simply have used the appelation by which the Jewish priest was commonly known.

4) תקרבת is the abbreviated form of תקרובתא . The Targum renders by it מנחה (Genesis 32:13; 20:21; Is. 18:7; Jer. 51:59 etc.).

5) It would seem that T. Jonathan did not follow at all such a distinction. So בעם קרבנם (Ez. 20:28) is rendered by T. Jon. קורבניהן unless the translator understood it in a holy sense.

6) In Tosefta Ab. Zara 2 there is מזבחין instead of מזבלין though in Pesiqta r. 6 רי"א יום זבול נילוס . The version in Sota 36b is

Moved with this spirit, the Targum is also differently
rendering Kohan according as the reference is to an Aaronite
or a priest of an idol. The latter is rendered by פלחא. (So Jer.
48:7; 49:3) or, which is the usual rendering, by כומרא (2K 10:19;
17:32 etc.) which is considered by some scholars to be a translation of the Persian Atharnan, the priest of the fire-worshippers.
(See Aruch, Kohut כמר) Both of them are found in the Talmud
and the Agada. The priest of the idol is called משרת (San. 63b,
64a). In one passage both of them are used side by side, namely
Erub. 79b. כומרא however is the usual connotation for the Kohan
of the idol. But 2S 8:18 ובני דוד כהנים the rendering is רברבין
(Com. Mech. יתרו 2,: ...כל כהנים מבטלים בענין, שנאמר ובני דור)
Com. Mek. l. c. וישמע יתרו : כהן מדין, ר' יהושע אומר כומר היה,
כענין שנאמר ויהונתן בן גרשם בן מנשה ובניו היו כהנים לשבט הדני

יום חגם היה, Com. also Cant. ı. beginning and Gen. ı. 87,3. The T.
Jon. in general does not favor any distinction in this case. Thus 1K 11:8·
ומזבחות לאלהיהן Targum ומדבחות . So also in 12:32; Am. 4:4 and
in some other places. So Onk. Num. 24:2 לזבחי אלהיהן ; לדבחי — זבחי
Deut. 32:17 יזבחו לשדים — דבחי . This principle found application
in the Bible. בשת is placed for בעל ; בית און for בית אל . This might
have been the reason for the peculiar vocalization of מקדשׁיחם (Ezek.
7:24), which is otherwise hardly explicable. (Com. Kimchi l. c.; Ew.
Gramm. 215 Jahn, Das Buch Ez. l. c.). The reference here is to the
idolatrous shrines (so Rashi, Kratezschmar and many others) and was
so understood by the Masorites. They therefore changed the pointing
as a mark of distinction. Similarly השׁיבו (Ezra 10:2; Nehemia 13:23)
instead of נשאו As in the judgment of the writer intermarriage is
an enormous violation of the Law, he would hesitate to use the word
commonly used for the act of taking to a wife.

The names of Gods should be changed into derogatory names
(R. Akiba in Sifri Deut. 61). Mockery of the idol was the rule with
the Hellenistic Jews also. It was for this reason that they applied the
εἰδωλόθυτος to what the G e n t i l e s called ἱερόθυτος
(Diessman, Die Hellen., p. 5). Likewise the idolatrous festival
is called איד (Abod. Zara 2a), and Maimonides (in his commentary on Mishnayoth) says: "and it is not allowed to call them
(the festivals of the idolators) מועדים because they are הבל " Com.
Rab, Aboda Zara 20a. A temple of an idol is called תרפות (Mishna
Ab. Zara 29b, 32b). Its underlying meaning is not from תורפה
(Aruch חרף), but synonymous with תרפות as Tos. (Ibid 32b beginning
החולך).

עד יום גלות הארץ; ר' אלעזר המודעי אומר שר היה, כענין שנאמר ובני דוד כהנים היו.

Also 2S 20:26 רב לדוד—וגם עידא היה כהן לדוד . The targumist does not consider them priests of any kind, although with regard to עירא the T. is in opposition to the view expressed in the Talmud (Erubin 63b) that he was a rightful priest. On the other hand, 1S 1:3 חפני ופנחס כהנים Targum משמשין obviously be-cause they were sinful priests, as against Samuel b. Nachmani, who would clear them of crime (Shab. 55b). Impelled by the same consideration, the T. renders הבמה (1S 9, 12, 13, 14, 25) by אסחרותא by which he renders מושבך (1S 20:18) and לשכתה (1S 9:22) to distinguish it from the bama denoting high places of idolatrous worship which he renders by במותא (1K 13:32; 14:23 etc.), having also the meaning of ruins. (Ez. 36:2). The targumist appears to decline the talmudic view (Zebachim 112b, 118a) that the ban of bama had been lifted at that time. In order to exonerate Samuel of the sin of bama-worship, the T. rendered הבמה as denoting the place where gatherings were held with the Prophet. Hence the rendering for יברך הזבח (1S 9:13) in the essenic sense [7] ארי הוא פרים מזונא (Ant. 1, 18, 5; Berakoth 55a), while 1S 16:3, 5 is equally rendered by בשירותא . For the same reason the T. renders תרפים (Jud. 17:5) by דמאין instead of צלמניא which is other-wise the rendering of תרפים (So On. Ps. Jon. Gen. 31:19). As well said Levy (Chal. Woer.): "Um nicht einem Jüdischen Priest die Anbetung eines hömlichen götzen Bildes zuzu-schreiben." So he differentiates in the rendering of אפוד . When it is used in a holy sense (1S 2:28) it is rendered אפוד but in a profane sense (1S 2:18; 2S 5:14) it is translated כרדוט רבוץ. This is the rendering of מעילים (2S 13:18). As regards other translations, the כומרא connotation for the priest of the idol is adopted by Onk. and P., while the Lxx makes no dinstinction.

Of the same character is the separation drawn by the targumist between משפט referring to that of God or Israel and that of the Gentiles. In the former case it is rendered by דינא.

---

7) Abudraham (שחרית ישתבח) cites a Targum Yerushalmi which would seem to be a later recenssion, this principle being disregarded. The rendering there is: ארי הוא יפרס על נכסא.

Referred to the משפט of the Gentiles or denoting custom it is rendered by the Greek νομὸς נימום . So Ez. 5:7 וכמשפטי הגוים — ואת משפטיהם אל תשמרו Ez. 20:18; וכנמוסי עממיא Targum וית נימוסיהן. Also Ez. 7:27; 21:25 and in one verse Ez. 11:12 וירעתם כי אני ר' אשר בחוקי לא הלכתם ומשפטי לא עשיתם ובמשפטי די בקימי לא הלכתון ודיני לא עבדתון וכנמוסי Targum הגוים עממיא. When משפט הכהנים denotes custom: 1S 2:13 מה משפט האיש (2K 1:7); נימום Targum משפט המלך וכו' (1S 8:9) נימום Targum וחי דרך באר-שבע Am. 8:14. Also נמוסא. Targum Applying to the holy laws, commandments or judgment it is rendered דינא Of this sort are Is. 1:27; 3:14; 5:7; Jer. 2:12; 22:3; Ez. 20:16; 12:21, 24. Sometimes suggested by Instances of both cases are numerous. On the other hand, משפט the contents דקשט truthful, is added. Instances of this kind are Jer. 5:1 אם ית עבוד דין דקשט Targum אם יש עשה משפט So vv. 4, 5; 7:5 אם מעבד תעברון Targum אם עשה תעשו משפט והבן משפט וצדקה עשה Ez. 18:19 Targum . דין דקשוט דין דקשוט עבד Targum והבן משפט וצדקה עשו Ez. 18:19. ויעביד דין דקשט Targum ועשה משפט and v. 21. It appears from the citations that the targumist adds דקשט when משפט is the object of עשה, did, or when this is understood by the targumist to be implied. (Jerem. 5:45). It might have appeared to him that to render משפט in these cases by דינא alone would be obscure, as it might be taken in a profane sense. In this connection it will be noticed that in a single case is משפט rendered by קימא, otherwise the rendering of חק as it will appear presently. This is Jer. 8:7. However, משפט there is also the object of עשה . The Lxx and P. in the Prophets are not following such a distinction. Onk. renders חק by נימום if it refers to Gentiles. So Lev. 20:23 etc., while otherwise חק, as is the case with Jonathan, is rendered by קימא . So Lev. 20:22; 26:3 etc.; the Lxx have for חק in holy sense προςτάγματος So ibid: 20:22; 26:3 etc.

While the profane חק ibid 2:23 is rendered by Lxx νομίμος In the Talmud this term is applied to custom, manner, judicial formatlity. (Com. Gittin 43b; 65b).

The same principle the targumist applies to חק . It is rendered by נזירא when it refers either to Gentiles or idolatrous law or order. When, however, it refers to the holy laws, it is rendered by קימא covenant (the usual rendering of ברית). Instances of the latter are : Jer. 31:35; Ez. 5:6; 18:9, 10, 19, 21; Am. 2:4; Ze. 1:6; Mal. 3:22 etc. Instances of the former are: Jer. 10:3 חקות העמים Targum גזירת ; 33:25 (חקות ירח וכוכבים) ; the same) נזירת Targum חקות שמים וארץ) (the same 33:34 חקות ירח וכוכבים) Ez. 20:18 בחקי אבותיכם אל תלכו Targum בנזירת ; 43:18 In Ez. 33:9 גזירת — לכל חקות 44:5 So. גזירת Targumאלה חקות בחקות — בנזירת חייא. In this way the T. renders Ez. 20:25 גזירן — וגם אני נתתי להם חוקים לא טובים·, thus eliminating the disturbing nature of this passage. According to this rendering of the T., the assumption is that also their customs (laws) were decreed by God. Concerning the use of גזירא it will be noticed that in the Talmud it has the effect of arbitrariness. So there are hard גזירות (Makkoth 24a; Ketuboth 3b; Shab. 145b). A גזירא can be recalled, Gittin 55b; Taanith 2 גזירא עבירא דבטלא ; to the targumist it appeared to express profanity. Apart from Jonathan, no other translation adhers in this case to such a distinction.[8]

The same principle is applied by Jonathan to the rendering of נביא In the case of the true prophet, the one sent by God, it is rendered by נביא , its Aramic equivalent. On the other hand, whenever it carries the implication of either false prophetism or, so to say, professional prophetism, נביא is rendered by ספר scribe, a term of general currency in the age of the Targum. So it renders Is. 9:14 ומנביא ועד ספר — Jer. 6:13 ונביא מורה שקר ומספר — כהן . Other examples of this sort are: Jer. 14:18; 18:18. In plural: Ez. 32:25 קשר נביאיה — סיעת ספראה. Ze. 7:3 בספריא—האף שאול בנביאים Note 1S 10:5 ולספריא — ואל הנביאים

When reference is made to a prophet of another deity, the targumist renders it literally, adding שקרא false. So Jer. 2:8 — והנביאים נבאו שקר; 5:31 נביי שקרא — והנביאים נבאו בבעל נביי שקרא; 1K 22:10 ·. הנביאים — נביי שקרא. וכל. To this cate- gory belongs also Mi. 2:5. There is annother case which is intimately connected with these cases. In the first place the T.

---

8) Kohut's identifying גזירא with חק as suggested by the render- ing of the T. (see Aruch גזר) is based on his overlooking the principle of distinction of the T.

applies the same distinction to the verb as well as to the noun. מתנבא referring to the true prophet is rendered by the T. איתנבי, referring to the false prophet it has a substitute ex-pressing ridicule. So Jer. 29:26 ומטפש — לכל איש ומתנבא (but v. 27 מתנבא). 1K 18:29 (מתנבא — למה גערת בירמיה העינתותי המתנבא). ואשטתיאו — ויתנבאו עד לעלות המחנה

In all these cases the Targum stands alone among other translations in observing such a differentiation.

Special regard has been paid in rendering by the targumist to Israel.[9] In the first place some harsh expressions flung towards Israel is rendered in such a way as to evaporate their sharpness. It should be remarked that in this the Targum is to some extent followed by all the Greek translations as well as the Peshitta. A few cases will be sufficient to illustrate the point.

The Piel from שוב in the sense of transgression is given a favorable turn when applied to Israel.[10]   So משבה ישראל (Jer. 3:6) is rendered by the T.   דמתחמנין למיתב לפולחני Lxx: κατοιϰία . So also P. In the same way T. Lxx P. in v. 8 A. Sym. ἡ ἀπος̣τροφὴ ἰσραήλ. In v. 11 the T. and P. are fol-lowing the same rendering while Lxx omit משבה . Again שובבים (v. 14)   T.   and   P.   render   as   in   former   cases,   Lxx

---

9) It is generally known that Jewish-Hellenistic writers, led, it would appear, by this principle, applied ἔθνος to the Gentiles, while retaining   λαὸς   for the Jewish people. (So Wisd. 15:14. Com. Cheyne, Encyc. Biblica, Hellen.). The Lxx followed the same division in an opposite way, applying the latter to the Gentiles. Com. Gen. 23:12, 13; 42:10 etc עם הארין — λαὸς τῆς γῆς. But Lev. 20, 2, 4 the rendering is τὸν ἔθνος , the reference being to Israel. Com. also 2 Mak. 6:3. In this connection it is of interest to note that Rashi somehow felt this peculiarity in the Targum. However, he is wrong in the illustration. Thus he remarks in Ze. 13:7: "the Targum never renders מלך ושרים when they are those of Israel except by רברב and not by שלטונין . It is first of all to be remarked that the ren-dering of שרים by רברבין is not peculiar to those of Israel. The same is applied to those of other nations also. Com. Is. 16:6; 34:6 (having both renderings used synonymously); Jer. 25:19; 39:3; 46:21, 23, and in many other instances. On the other hand we find שלטונין applied to those of Israel. So Is. 37:24 etc.

10) This is also the case in Onk. (Com. Deut. 32:6 the ren-dering of עם נבל ולא חכם . See A. Berliner, Onk. p. 120.)

having ἀφεστηκότες ; Sym. ῥεμβόμενοι. V. 22 שובו בנים
תובו בניא דמתחמנין .T is rendered by שובבים ארפה משובתכם
למיתב אשבק לכון כד תתובון .

משבותיכם, however, is rendered by the Lxx affliction (so that
there is no reason to ascribe to the Lxx a different reading; com. Schlesner Lexicon σύντριμμα). Also ib. 5:6, 31:32.
Exceptions are: Jer. 2:19; 14:17, where Lxx render in the
unfavorable sense. T a r g u m and P. hold to the above
rendering.

The same word is rendered in its intended sense when
it refers to other nations than Israel. Note Jer. 49:4 הבת השובבה
(referring to Amon) T. מלכותא טפשתא , Lxx θυγατερ ἰταμίας
audacious. Also Is. 47:10 חכמתך ורעתך היא שובבתך — קלקלתך
Is. 57:17 forms an exception, although the reference is made
to refer to Israel, the rendering by the T. and Lxx is plain. So
strong, it appears, was the force of suggestion of the contents
of this particular case that it was felt impossible to make other
account of it. [11]

In the following case the T. is followed by Aquila in some
measure. Ez. 2:10   ויפרוש אותה לפני וכתוב אליה קינים והגה והי
the T., apparently disturbed by the vehemency of the prophecy,
renders : וכתיב בה דאם יעברון בית ישראל על אוריתא ישלטון בהון
עממיא וכד יעבדון ית אוריתא יסוף מנהון אליא ודינא ותינחתא.
In this way the gloomy predcition is turned into one of consolation. A., it seems, was also actuated by the same motive,
rendering קינים — c r e a t i o n (probably from the root
קנא) ; com. also Is. 28:9; 56:3; Hos. 13:14.

In his regard for Israel the T. goes farther to differentiate
them from other peoples. Here are some interesting examples:
Jer. 1:10 ראה הפקדתיך היום הזה על הגוים ועל הממלכות לנתש ולנתיץ
ולהאביד ולהרס — the T. divides the phrase, assigning its favorble
part to Israel חזי דמניתיך יומא הדין על עממיא ועל מלכותא לתרעא.

___

11)   Kimchi's Sefer Ha-Sharashim, after enumerating all the cases
which the targumist as well as the Greek translations and the P. render
them by its favorable meaning, remarks: "all these mean rebellion."
In this point he follows Menachem Ibn Saruck. (Com. Machbereth שוב).
In Machbereth Rabeinu Tam (Ed. Pilpowsky) p. 36, it is said: Hos. 8:6
כי שובבים יהיה the sinful man is called שובב , being removed from
the good direction.

ועל בני ישראל למבני ולקימא ולאברא ולפגרא . Nothing but a passion-
ate regard for Israel could have produced such a rendering.
Com. Is. 10:25; Jer. 18:7.[12] This scrupulous passion for Israel
is accompanied by a kind of active disregard for the gentiles.
It was the product of the catastrophies of the age. Thus the
targumist is aghast at the idea that the prophet should be overcome by the c a l a m i t i e s of other peoples. For
this reason he changes the person, and instead of the prophet
agonizing for sympathy, as the text requires, the peoples involved
are describing their sufferings. So, for instance, Is. 15:5 :
לבי למואב יזעק ; Is. 16:11; Jer. 48:36 Targum בלבהון יימרון
; על כן מעיהון דמואבי ולבהון... Targum על כן מעי למואב ככנור יהמו
Is. 21:3 : על כן מלאו מתני חלחלה צירים אחזוני כצירי יולדה נעויתי
על כן איתמליאו חרציהון זיעיא דחלא Targum משמע נבהלתי מראות
תעה לבבי פלצות : 4 .and v אחדתינון אטפשו מלשמע טעו מלמיחזי
טעא לבהון עקא וביעותין Targum בעתתני את נפש חשקי שם לי לחרדה
אחרונון אתר רוחצניהון היה להון לתבר . In some instances he re-
tains the p. but alters the sense. Examples of this sort are :
Is. 16:9; Jer. 48:32 על כן אבכה בבכי יעזר גפן שבמה אריוך דמעתי
על כן כמא דאיתיתי משרין על יעזר כן איתי קטולין על שבמה Targum
אריינך דמעתא   But otherwise is such a case treated by the
targumist when Israel is meant. The prophet's description of
his feelings towards the affliction of Israel is rendered literally.
So Is. 22:4 על כן אמרתי שעו מני אמרר בבכי אל תאיצו לנחמני על
על כן אמרית שבוקו מני אבכי במרר לא תתבעיתו Targum שוד בת עמי
לנחמותי על תבר כנשתא דעמי.
    The Lxx are in agreement with the Targum in the render-
ing of Is. 15:5 and Jer. 48:31 and v. 36. The Syriac in all
these cases follows the literal meaning. The fact that Aq. and
Sym. have instead of the rendering of the Lxx of vv. 31, 36
one which is literal strengthens the supposition that the renderings of the Lxx in these cases were caused by the same motives
as lead the targumist to his. However, there is less consistence
in the Lxx with regard to this point. Com. Lxx Is. 16:9, 11.

---

12) Kimchi remarks: "And Jonathan divided this verse—the unfavorable for the Gentiles and the favorable for Israel." In the present
Rabbinic text the למבני ישראל is omitted, evidently by the censor. Com.
Exod. r. 45, 1 רגע אדבר על גוי אלו ישראל... ועל ממלכה אלו ישראל...
לנתש... לפי שעשו אותו מעשה ובקש להשמידם.

On the other hand, this peculiar agreement between the Lxx and the Targum is another case of weight for an hypothesis of a common background of these translations.

However, Geiger (Ur. 245 et seq.), who carried this principle too far, failed to notice these renderings. He was most unfortunate in the choice of examples. Thus his assertion (p. 93) that Jer. 48:47 ; 49:6, where the restoration of Moab and Ammon is foretold, are not rendered in the Lxx, is errone- ous, for the lost renderings are found in Gmg.

Other examples are: Jer. 8:23; 13:17; 14:17; Mi. 4:5 etc. Com. particularly Ze. 8:2. Other agadists would not follow this interpretation. Com. Num. r. 20, 1. The targumist would not have been actuated by a hatred towards the respective peoples; Edom and Moab have ceased to exist at his time. It is more correct to take it as the reaction of the age against the Roman world. It is the deep-seated hatred of the time immediately preceding and following the destruction of the second Temple. It was the Prophetical writings where that generation looked for the signs of the times. The prophecies were interpreted in the terms of that period. The old oppressors of Israel, long dead, were revived in the new oppressors. Edom and Aram be- come Rome or Persia. Compassion by the prophet towards the biblical enemies would strike them as if their present oppressors were meant. Such would be horrible to them.

The targumist shares in full measure the worshipful venera- tion of the Torah manifested in the Talmud and Agada. The Torah is given by him prominence in the Prophetical books. The Torah is identified with words descriptive, in the sense they are employed, of qualities representing the will of God. The targumist is again reflecting current views which are to be found in the Agada. דעת is identified by the T. with the Torah. Is. 40:14 ילמדהו דעת Targum אוריתא [13) ; ib. 28:9 את מי יורה דעת Targum עברי אוריתא (Hos. 6:6). Connected with it is Am. 3:10 לא ידעו עשות נכוחה ; Is. 30:10 לא תחזו לנו

---

13) Com. Alef Beitha of R. Akiba A'in: "and she ,the Torah, is called דעת , as it is written" etc.

אורח IS. 2:3; Mi. 4:2 נכחות Targum אולפן אוריתא . So also
מורא [14]; Mal. 2:5 באולפן אוריתיהן Targum נלכה באורחותיו
Targum באור יי Is. 2:5; אולפן אוריתי Targum ואתנם לי מורא
ובאוריתא Targum ואת פעל יי לא יביטו ib. 5:12; [15] באולפו אוריתי
אוריתא [16] Targum ותהי המשרה על שכמו ib. 9:5; לא אסתכלו
Hos. 10:12 אולפן אוריתא Targum נירו לכם ניר; Jerem. 4:5
אוריתא Targum שמר אמונים Is. 26:2; אוריתא Targum שברו עול
אוריתי [17]; Targum יחזיק במעוזי ib. 27:5; נאמנה Hos. 5:9); (So
Jer. 32:6 ומשקה צמא יחסור Targum [18] לפתגמי אוריתי (Com. Is.
55:1); Ze. 13:1 מקור נפתח Targum אולפן אוריתא יהי   In their
related positions, whether those cases occur in metaphor or are
simply conceived, they carry the significance of the all-conceived
good which Israel is urged by the Prophet to follow. It was
natural for the T., as it was the case with his contemporary
agadists, to identify them with the Torah.

The Torah thus gains centrifugal force in the prophecy.
On the observances or disregard of its precepts hinges the fate
of the nation; they are punished because they transgressed the
Torah (Am. 9:1; Jer. 11:16; 5:22 etc.). Other peoples suffer
for their failure to accept the Torah (Mi. 5:14). On the other
hand, Israel forsaking the Torah ceases to be God's people
(Hos. 1:9; 2:1; Zef. 2:1). Repentance forstalls calamity, but
this repentance is the return to the Torah (Is. 12:1; 31:7;
Jer. 31:18; Ez. 34:1).

In this connection it is worth while noticing the Halakic
element in the T. Jonathan. Of course, compared with the Pent.,
there is not much of Halaka in the Prophetical writings. But
in a few cases, which are especially accessible to Halakic interpretation, the targumist follows the interpretation of the Halaka.
All these cases occur in Ez.; the first is Ez. 24:17 פארך חבוש לראשך

14) Com. Jalqut l. c.: "Who accepted the words of the Torah
with fear."
15) Com. Midrash Shochar Tob (49): "R. Aba says, sweet
are the words of the Torah likened to אור etc."
16) Com. Jalqut (prov. 8): "By me princes will ישרו
(prov. 8:16), both the crown of priesthod an kingship come from
the power of the Torah."
17) Com. Zeb. 116a.
18) Com. B. Kama 17a; Canticles r. 1.

The Targum renders טוטפות—פאר (Tephilin). This is in accordance with Sukka 25b: "Said R. Aba b. Zabada : A mourner
has to observe all the commands of the Torah except Tephilin; for (this is to be inferred) because God said to Ez.
פארך חבוש עליך , you are obliged to observe it while a mourner,
but no other mourner is to observe it."
Ez. 44:17 Targum על אלהין חרציהון על יזרזון ולא
לא יחגרו ביזע לבבהון ייסרון . This agrees with the Beraith Zebachim 18b (end):
"They (the priests) do not girt below their loins but against
the knuckles."

Finally there is Ez. 44:22 והאלמנה אשר תהיה אלמנה מכהן יקחו
Targum וארמלתא די תהי ארמלתא שאר כהניא יסבון. This interpretation removes the flagrant contradiction which this interdiction presents to Lev. 3:17. It is so interpreted in Kid. 78b
משאר כהניא יקחו — מכהן יקחו.

The Messianic hope occupies a prominent place in the
exegesis of this Targum. In addition to the Messianic sense
which the targumist is giving to passages admittedly accessible
to such a conception, he introduces the Messianic note in many
a passage that is scarcely allowing itself of such an impliation.
The targumist is following the current interpretation of that age
of intense expectation.

In his Messianic interpretation the targumist had preserved many of the current ideas about the last days. On the
whole, they are identical with the Messianic description contained in the Apocryphal books, Enoch and 4 Ezra
and the Agada. The rectification of the evils of the world will
be completed on the Day of Judgment. The evil doers are given
respite in this world so that they may repent and turn to the
Torah (Hab.3:1, 2; Zef. 2:1, 2). But on the Day of Judgment
stern judgment will be meted out to the evil doers. There will be
no intercession and no escape (Is. 5:30. Com. 4 Ezra 7, 105; On.
Deut. 32:12). After the closing of the decree (the Day of Judgment) there will be no acceptance of repentance (Is. 8:22). The
world will be renewed (Jer. 23:23; Hab. 3:2. Com. Ps. Jon.
Deut. 32:1). Great wonders and miracles will appear, as in the
time of the Exodus from Egypt (Hos. 21:66; Ze. 10:11). The
Messiah, who was created from the beginning of the world and
who was hidden from the world on account of the sins of the

poeple (Mi. 4:8; 5:1; Zech. 4:7; 6:12. Com. Enoch 48, 3, 6; 62, 7)
will appear. There will be a resurrection of the death. It seems
the targumist expects both the righteous and the wicked to re-
surrect, the former to receive final judgment. (Com. Is. 38:16;
42:11; 45:8, and particularly 57:16. Com. Enoch 51, 2, 3). The
Great Court will sit to judgement (2S 23:7), the wicked will die a
second death (IS. 22:14; 65:6; Jer. 51:39, 57; com. Enoch 22, 6-
12; the Syr. Baruch 76, 4), they will be thrown in Gehenna (Is.
33:17; 53:9; Jer. 17:13; Hos. 14:10), whose fire is burning always
(Is. 65:5). In Jerusalem will the wicked be condemned to
Gehenna (Is. 33:14; com. Enoch 90:20). The righteous ones will
live the life of eternity חיי עלמא (Is. 58:11; Hos. 14:10); they will
shine 343 times (7x7x7), as the light of the seven stars in the
seven days of creation (Judges 5:31; 2S 23:4; Is. 30:26; the
extant edition of the Tanchuma Gen. 6 cites the Targum to
Judges 5:31). Com. Tanchuma ed. Buber, Gen. note 143.

INTERPOLATED TARGUM

The composite nature of T. Jonathan has been definitely demonstrated above. The T. did not escape the peculiar fate of the Greek and Syriac versions, which were preyed upon by later editors, forcing into them other material. It was all the more so an inevitable procedure with the T. Its original purpose to be merely an instrument for the instruction of the ignorant; its place in the public worship; its varied history of wandering were strong factors in rendering it susceptible to changes. It was exposed to the irresistible influences of the Midrash, which thrived in the immediate centuries following the destruction of the Second Temple. Later Midrashim crowded into the original, simple exegesis of Jonathan. The new material caused in many cases a mutilation of the original rendering, thus becoming either obscure or an overflowing rhetoric. Such portions contrast sharply with the close, smooth, natural rendering of Jon. The Midrashic incursion is especially remarkable in the first 35 chapters of Isaiah. One need only read the T. to Jerem. or Ezekiel to be impressed by the curious difference. But in most all these cases it is impossible to release the original from the new form. In some instances the translation may represent a completely new rendering which replaced the older one. Few additions can be safely pointed out. Some of them will be found to be two different renderings put side by side. As it is generally known, duplicates of this kind are found in the ancient versions, Onkelos included. We will begin with the major portions, presenting Midrashic portions which have made inroads into the T. Jonathan.

בד מרדו בית —– בפרע פרעות בישראל בהתנדב עם Judges 5:2
ישראל באוריתא אתו עליהון עממיא וטרדונון —– וכד תבו למעבד
אוריתא אתנברון אינון על בעלי דבביהון ותרכינון מכל (מעל) תחום ארעא
דישראל —– בכן על פורענות תבר סיסרא וכל מישריתיה ועל נסא ופורקנא

126

ראתעביד להון לישראל, — בכן תבו חכימיא למתב בבתי כנשתא בריש
גלי ולאלפא ית עמא פתגמי אוריתא; בכן ברוכו ואורו.

The T. to this verse contains three different renderings
to the second half of the v. One interpreting it as implying that
when the people return to the Torah they overcome their enemies
and expel them from the land of Israel; the other taking it to
refer to the overthrow of Sisra; the third to the deliverance
from the prohibition on the study of the Law, the targumist
having in mind the Hadrian persecutions. It is hardly possible
to determine which is the older one. But the latter persisted
in v. 9. המתנדבים בעם.

Com. Seder Eliahu r. 11 (p. 52): ובדו יאי להון דיתבין בבתי
כנשתא ומאלפין ית עמא פתגמי אוריתא. במי הקב"ה נפרע מאומות
העולם? בבני אדם שהן משביעין ומערבין לבית הכנסת שנאמר . . .
המתנדבים בעם ומברכים את הקב"ה.

שמעו מלביא—ראתו עם סיסרא לקרבא;—שמעו מלבים ib. 3
אציתא שלטיניא — דהוו עם יבין מלכא דכנען — לא בחלתיכון ולא
בנבורתכון אתגברתון וסלקתון על בית ישראל.

The two portions following the horizontal line are missing in
Cod. Reuch. and in Ant. Polyg. and preceded by תום' in ed.
Leira, and appear in brackets in the London Polyg. and in the
Basel ed.

— אוריתא דיהבתא לישראל עלה — יי בצאתך משעיר... ib. 4
הוה שלטין בהון עממיא וכד תיבין לה מתגברין אינון על בעלי דבביהון,
ביום אתגליותך למתנה להון . . .

The intrusive character of the portion is obvious. It belongs
to v. 2 and is a recenssion of the first rendering. It is missing
in the Ant. Polyg.

טוריא זעו מן קדם יי— טורא דתבור,— הרים נזלו מפניו ib. 5
טורא דחרמון וטורא דכרמלא ואמרין דין לדין, דין אמר עלי תשרי
שכינתיה ולי חזיא ודין לדין אמר עלי תשרי שכינתיה ולי חזיא —
(מקראות גדולות, אמשטרדם, תפ"ו), אשרי שבנתיה על טוריא רסיני
דהוא חלש וזעיר מכל טוריא — דין סיני מתרגיש . . .

It is a shortened form of the Targum on the margin of Cod.
Reuch containing a current Agada (Com. Gen. r. 99, 1) cited
in Jalqut from Jelamdenu. Refrence to this Agada is made in
T. to PS 68:16, 17. That it is an interpolation is shown in the

London Polyg., where the whole portion is placed in brackets,
while in Cod. Reuch the addition is found והוה רעווא מן קדם יי
ואשרי שכינתיה. It is completely omitted in Ed. Leira and in the
Ant. Polyg.

כד איתרעו בני ישראל למפלח לטעוותא — יבחר אלהים 8 .ib
חדתין — וכד תבו למעבר אוריתא לא יכילו להון עד דאיתגברין
וסליק עליהון סיסרא סנאה ומעיקא. בארבעין אלפין רישי משירין בחמשין
אלפין אחרי סיפא בשתין אלפין אחרי תריסין בתמנן אלפין מחצצי גיריא
בר מתשע מאה רתכין דברזלא דהוו עמיה כל אלין אלפיא וכל
אלין משיריתא לא יכלון למקם קדם ברק וקדם עשרה אלפין גברא דעימיה...
There cannot be the slightest doubt that this Agada was on
the margin to v. 2, the end of which formed על פורענות סיסרא
וכל משריתיה of v. 2, which is strikingly out of all connection.
Witness the beginning וכד תבו of v. 2. It was by a marginal
mistake that it was introduced here, where it has no room. As
to its source, com. Jalqut l. c. It appears in a shortened form
in Cod. Reuch., where the version is as follows:

וכד תבו לאוריתא לא יכילו להון דכר אתא עליהון שטאה ועימיה אחרי
תריסין ורומחין בארבעין אלפין רישי משיריין לא יכילו לאגתא קרבא
בישראל.
In Ed. Leira it is headed by: תוספתא

מאתר דהוי אנסין להון — מקול מחצצים בית משאבים 11 .ib
ונסבין מה בידיהון בית מכונת (כמנת) לסטין ומתובת מוכסין על נובין
בית שקיא דמיא — לאתר דהוון נפקין בנת-ישראל לממלי מיא דלא הואה
יכלין (דחלין) לאישמעא קל (טרפת) פרסת רגלאי מן קדם (כמנת) סנאה
Is is a second rendering. It is omitted in Cod. Reuch. In Leira
ed. it is preceded by the following addition:

אתרא דאיתעבידא להון נסין וגבורן לדבית ישראל מלקדמין אתר . . .

למה תבתון ממשרית קרבא — למה ישבת בין המשפתים 16 .ib
למתב בין תחומין — בפרשת אורחא למשמע בשורתא דא מן דא לברק
אתון אמרין דילך אנחנא לסיסרא אתון אמרין דילך אנחנא כי למשמע
בשורא .
This interpretation might have been intended to deal a rebuke
to the half-hearted revolutionists of the Saducean party in the
Great Rebellion. It is omitted in Cod. Reuch. and in ed. Leira it
is headed 'תוספ ; the rendering בין תחומין — בין המשפתים
agrees with Onk. and Ps. Jon., Gen. 49:14.

ib. 26 טבתא יעל אשת חבר שלמאה דקימת—ירדה ליתר תשלחנה

מה דכתיב בספר אוריתא דמשה לא יהוי תיקון דגבר על אתתא ולא יתקן

גבר בתיקוני אתתא אלהין ידא לסכתא . . .

It is a current interpretation in a shortened form. Com. Jalqut
l. c. (cited from Midrash Achbar):

ידיה שלחה בכישור זו יעל שלא הרגתו בכלי זיין אלא ביתר דכתיב ידה

ליתד . . . ומפני מה לא הרגתו בכלי זיין ? לקיים מה שנאמר לא יהיה

כלי גבר על אשה.

This addition is missing in Cod. Reuch., and in the Ant. Polyg.;
in ed. Leira it is headed by תוס׳ .

ib. 11:1 רא היא נימוסא הות בישראל מלקדמין דלא מסתחרא

אחסנתא משבטא לשבטא ובכן לא היה יבול גבר למיסב

אתתא דלא הות משבטיה וכדהות אתתא דרחימת גברא הות נפקא מבי נשא

בלא אחסנתא והון אנשין קרין לה פונדקיתא דרחימת גברא דלא מישבטא

ובן הות לה לאימיה דיפתח.

This Targum is cited by Kimchi l. c. and is found in ed. Leira
under heading "Tosefta" No other edition has it.

ib. 39 והואה לגזירה בישראל — בדיל דלא — ותהי לחק בישראל

לאסקה גבר ית בריה וית ברתיה לעלתא במה דעבד יפתח גלעדאה דלא

שאיל לפנחס כהנא, ואילו שאיל לפנחס כהנא הוה פריק יתה בדמין.

It appears in a different version on the margin of Cod. Reuch.
to 12:7. The essence of this Agada is found in Gen. r. 60, 1,
holding to the view of R. Jochanan that a vow of this sort
should be redeemed by money. This author also condemns Jef-
tah for not going to Pinehas to ask the disavowal. Others think
the reverse is true. Com. Seder Eliahu r. 12 (p. 55). This portion
beginning בדיל is found in the Leira ed. headed by "Tosefta"
and is missing in the Ant. Polyg.

IS 2:1 וצלאית חנה ברוח — ותתפלל חנה ותאמר עלץ לבי ביי

נבואה ואמרית רמי קרני בי׳ — כבר שמואל ברי עתיד למהוי נביא על

ישראל ביומוהי יתפרקון מירא דפלשתאי ועל ידוהי יתעברון להון נסין

ונבורן בכן ; תקיף לבי בחולקא דיהב לי ; ואף הימן בר ברי שמואל

(רהי״א ו : ח) עתיד דיקום הוא וארבע עשר בנוהי למהוי אמרין בשירה

על ידי נבלין וכינורין עם אחיהון לויאי לשבחא בבית מקדשא בכן ;

רמה קרני במתנתא דמני לי יי — ואף על פורענות ניסא דעתיד להוי

בפלישתאי דעתידרון דייתון ית ארונא דיי׳ בעגלתא חדתא ועמיה קורבן

אשמא בכון תימר כנשתא דישראל : אפתח פומי . . .

The whole portion is missing in the Ant. Polyg.

The additions appear with minor modifications in all editions.
In the Basel ed. and the London Polyg., however, they are
placed in brackets. As to the interpretation that Hanna was
prophesying, com. Meg. 14a.

על סנחירב מלכא דאתור איתנביאת ואמרת — אין קדוש   ib. 2
עתיד דיקום הוא ובל חילותיה על ירושלם ונם סני יתעביד ביה תמן יפלון
פגרי משריתיה בבן יודן כל עממיא אומיא ולישניא ויימרון לית קדוש...
The whole addition is missing in the Ant. Polyg. and appears
in the Basel ed. and the London Polyg. in brackets.

על נבוכדנצר מלכא דבבל איתנביאת ואמרת — ואל תרבו   ib. 3
אתון כסדאי וכל עממיא דעתידין למשלט ביישראל ; לא תסגון . . .
It is missing in the Ant. Polyg. and appears in brackets in the
Basel ed. and the London Polyg.

על מלכות יון איתנביאת ואמרת — יתברון—קשת גברים   ib. 4
קשתת דגברי יונאי ; ודבית חשמונאי : דהוו חלשין . . .
In the Basel ed. and in the London Polyg. these portions are
in brackets, and are omitted in the Ant. Polyg.

על בנוהי דהמן איתנבאית ואמרת : דהוו — שבעים בלחם   ib. 5
שבעין בלחמא — מרדכי ואסתר : בן ירושלים דהות כאתתא עקרא . . .
ורומי . . . יסופון משריה — תצדי ותחרבי.
In the Basel ed. and in the London Polyg. these portions are
in brackets. Instead of רומי it has ארם, an intentional change,
for obvious reasons, and are missing in the Ant. Polyg.

אלהי צורי אחסה בו מגני וקרן ישעי משגבי ומנוסי —   2S 22:2
אלהי דאתרעי בי קרבני לדחלתיה תוקפי דמן קדמוהי מתיהבת לי תקוף
ופורקן לאתגברא על בעלי דבבי דוחצני — דעל מימריה אנא רחין ואמר
לארמא קרני בפורדקניה סומכני דהוה מימרי סמוך לי — כדהויתי עריק...
This portion is missing in the Targum to Ps. That the
portion is a second and different rendering to the second half
of the verse, is evident. Its other part to the first half seems to
have been included in the first rendering. In the Ant. Polyg.
the portion ראתרעי בי קרבני לדחלתיה is omitted.
As to the rendering of צורי Com. IS 2:2; 2S 22:47, On. Deut.
32:4. And וקרן Com. IS 2:1. All of which would lend strength
to this supposition.

טוביכון צדיקיא עבדתון לכון עובדין — וכאור בקר   ib. 23:4
טבין... — על חד תלת מאה ארבעין ותלתא כניהור שבעת יומיא יתיר
מכרין תתדבון ויטב לכון דהויתון מחמדין ליֹשני נחמתא דאתיין — הא...

This part is missing in the Ant. Polyg. This is another indication that the Targum to this verse belongs to a Midrashic T.
which was by a later editor incorporated in the T. and which
displaced the original T. In the text used by Montanus it appeared in a shortened form. Com. Cod. Reuch., Judges 5:8.

בכן על ניסא ופורקנא דיתעביד למשיחך — כי מי אל 32 .ib
ולשארא דעמך דאישתארון יודון כל עממיא ויישניא ויימרון : לית אלהא...
It is an addition. The same appears in a shortened form in the
T. to 1S 2:2, which in the London Polyg. is found in brackets.
It is missing in the Ant. Polyg.

בכן על ניסא ופורקנא דעבדתא לעמך בית ישראל — חי יי 47 .ib
אודיאו ואמרו קים . . .
It is another form of v. 32. Is is missing in the Ant. Polyg.
and in the T. to Ps.

וידבר על העצים מן הארז אשר בלבנון ועד האזוב 4:33 1K —
ואיתנבי על מלכי בית דוד דעתידין למישלט בעלמא דין ובעלמא דאתי
דמשיחא.
It is a Midrashic interpretation which can in no way be read
into the verse. Had it represented the original of the T., the
same interpretation would have been applied to the second part
of the v. But the latter is rendered literally. However, the original
was displaced by the toseftoic rendering. The displaced original
is found in the Ant. Polyg.; the rendering there is as follows:
ומליל על אעיא מארזא די בלבנן ועד אזובא דנפק בכותלא ומלל על
בעירא ועל עופא ועל רחשא ועל נוניא.

ואתתא חדא מנשי — ואשה אחת מנשי בני הנביאים 4:1 2K
תלמידי נביאייה מצוחא קדם אלישע למימר עבדך עובדיה בעלי מית
ואת ידעת ארי עבדך הוה דחיל מן קדם יי' דכד קטלת איזבל ית נביא
דיי' דבר מנהון מאה נובדין ואטמרינון חמשין חמשין גברא במערתא
והוה יזיף ומוכיל להון בדיל דלא לאכלותהון מנכסיה דאחאב מן קדם
דאינון אונסא וכען נשיא אתא למסב ית תרין בני ליה לעברין מתן ושתין
וחמשא זמנין צוווחת את עובדיה בהאי גוונא ולא הוה משגח ולא ידעה
מה למעבד לה עד דאזלא לבי קברי וצוחא דחלא דיי' ואשתמע לה קלא
מביני מיתיא מאן הדין דחלא ר' דקא בעית ארבעה איקרו דחלא ר'
אברהם יוסף ואיוב ועובדיה מתיבא ואמרה לא בעינא אלא היך דכתיב
ביה דחלא דיי לחדא וכד אורעיה קבריה הוה קא מתפלשא בעפריה
וקא צווחא ואמרה מרי מרי היכא רוח צריך לי בשעתא דמותא כי אמרית

לך למאן את שביק לי אתיבתני ריבון עלמא רחיץ לי ואמר לי שבוק יתמך
ואנא איקיימינון וארמלתך עלי תתדחץ ובדו לא נהשבחת משיזיב ויתמי
נמי צוחי ואמרי קבלת אבא אבא קבלן אבא, אתיב עובדיה ואמר לה זילי ליך
לגבי אלישע בפורתא דמשחא דאישתאר גביך ולברכוך ביה דאנא כד
אטמרתינהו למאה נביא וזנתיה במערתא בלחמא ובמיא לא איטפיין בו
ציני דמשחר מיניהו לא ביממא ולא בליליא לי דכר ליה נביא מילי בידי
לקודשא בריך הוא וישלים לכון מה דאוזפיתיה דהכי אמר קרא מוזיף
למרי עלמא כל מן דרחים על מסכינא ובכן אזלת ואורעתיד לאלישע
בולי האי.

This Tosefta is found in the edition Leira, which is also cited
by Kimchi (l. c.). All editions contain only the beginning of
this Tosefta without any indication of any sort to show its
toseftoic character. Here again an instructive example is presented to show how the toseftoic material was handled by later
editors. Such can be surmised was the case with other material
incorporated in the Targum but whose source we are unable
to trace. Com. Otzar Tov, v. 1, p. 10, Berlin, 1878.

Is. 10:32   עד היום בנב לעמד — עד כאן יומא רב וסני עדן

ליה למיעל הא סנחרב מלכא דאתור נטל ועבר תלת אונים ודבר עמיה
ארבעין אלפין גוספנין דדהב רבני מלכין קטירי תגא יתבין בהון ודבר
עמיה מאתן אלפין אחדי סיפין ורומחין דבר עמיה מאתן ושיתין אלפין
מחצצי גירין גוברין דרהטין קדמוהי מאה אלפין אורבא דמשריתיה ארבע
מאה פרסין, צואר סוסותיה ארבעין פרסין, מנין משריתיה מאתן ושתין
אלפין ריבוא חסר חד וכן אתו על אברהם כד רמו יתיה לגו נורא יקדתא
וכן עתידין למיתי עם גוג ומגוג כד ישלח עלמא קצי למתפקרא משריתא
קדמיתא כד עברו בירדנא שתו מיא דהוו בירדנא משריתא תניתא כד
עברו בירדנא חפרו בירין ושתו מיא אתא וקם בנוב קרית כהנא לקביל
שור דירושלם ועני ואמר לחילותיה הלא דא קרתא ירושלם דעלה ארגישית
כל משריתי ועלה כבישית כל מדינתי הא היא זעירא וחלשא מכל
כרכי עממיא דכבישית בתקוף ידי עלה קם מניד ברישיה מוביל ומיתי
בידיה על טור בית מקדשא...

All older Rabbinic editions contain this Midrashic Targum.
In the recent editions the part beginning מלכא and ending with
מיא   is placed in brackets. It is omitted in Cod. Reuch. and
in the Ant. Polyg. It appears on the margin of Cod. Reuch.
in an enlarged form.

In a somewhat modified form it is told in San. 95b :
אמר רב יהודה אמר רב בא עליהם סנחריב בארבעים וחמשה אלף איש

בני מלים ויושבים בקרנות של זהב ועמהם שגלונות וזונות ובשמונים
אלף גבורים לבושי שריון קליפה ובששים אלף אחוזי חרב רצים לפניו
והשאר פרשים וכן באו על אברהם וכן עתידין לבא עם גוג ומגוג.
בתניתא תנא אורך מחנהו ת' פרסא רוחב צואר סוסיו ארבעים פרסה
סך מחנהו מאתים וששים רבוא אלפין חסר חד . . . תנא ראשונה
עברו בשתי . . . אמצעים עברו בקומה . . . אחרונים העלו עפר על רגליהם
ולא מצאו מים בנהר לשתות עד שהביאו מים ממקום אחר.
Com. also Seder Eliahu r. 8 (p. 45). They represent two versions
of a current Agada. But the following portion containing Senacherib's address is also toseftoic. It is cited in the Aramaic in
San. 95a. Furthermore, it even has the complementary portion
which was dropped at its introduction in the T.

התשכח אשה עולה מרחם בן בטנה, גם אלה תשכחנה ib. 49:15
— האפשר דהתנשי אתתא ברה מלרחמא על בר מעהא — מתיבא כנישתא
דישראל ואמרת אם לית קדמוהי אתנשאה דלמא לא מתנשי לי ית דעבדית
ענג דרהב. אמר לה נביא אף אלין אתנשיא : מתיבא ואמרא (ואמרת)
ליה אם אית קדמוהי אתנשאה דלמא מתנשי לי ית דאמרית בסיני נעביד
ונקבל ואמר לה מימרי לא ירחקינך.

      So in Berakoth 34b :

אמר הקב"ה כלום אשכח עולות אילים ופטרי רחמים, שהקרבת לפני
במדבר ? אמרה לפניו רבש"ע הואיל ואין שכחה לפני כסא כבודך שמא
לא תשבח לי מעשה ענל ? אמר לה גם אלה תשכחנה. אמרה לפניו
רבש"ע הואיל ויש שכחה לפני כסא כבודך שמא תשכח לי מעשה סיני ?
אמר לה ואנכי לא אשכחך.

It appears from this that a part of this Midrash was dropped
by the interpolator. The first and last are remnants of the original
Targum. It is omitted in Cod. Reuch. and First Bomberger
ed. (Com. Bacher Z. D. M. G., p. 48.)

אמרת ירושלים האפשר דיתנסיב מעשו רשיעא ib. 24, 25
דאמיר עליה על חרבך תחי עדאה דעדי מני ואם שביא דשבא ישמעאל
דאמיר עליה דצדיקא היא ישתיזיב ? ארי כדנן אמר יי' אף עדאה דעדא
מניך עשו נברא יתנסב מניה ושביא רשבא מניך ישמעאל גיותנא דאמיר
עליה ערור באנשא ישתיזיב — וית פורענתיך...

The latter presents an excellent example of how a combination
of this sort was accomplished. The last portion is the original
Targum, upon which was built the Midrashic interpolation.
Both portions, which unquestionably belong somewhere in the
Geonic age, appear in the current editions after the orginal and

literal rendering under the heading תא . They appear on the margin of the Cod. Reuch. under the same name, being omitted in the text; while in the first Bom. ed. they appear in a shortened form in the T. to Is. 66:5 (Bacher, p. 20).

ib. 50:10, 11 . . . מי בכם ירא — אמר נביא עתיד קודשא בריך

הוא למהוי אמר לעממיא, מן בכון . . . מתיבין עממיא ואמרין קדמוהי רבוננא לא אפשר לגא למעסק באוריתא ארי כל ימנא אתגרינא דין עם (על) דין בקרבא וכד נצחנא דין לדין אוקידנא בתיהון ושביגא (נשיהון) טפלהון ונכסיהון ובחדא גונא שלימו יומנא ולא אפשר לנא למעסק באוריתא, מתיב קודשא בריך הוא ואמר להון כ' הא בולבון . . .

It is a satire particularly on Rome and Persia. Com. Aboda Zara 2b. In most all editions these portions are placed in brackets. They are missing in Cod. Reuch. and First Bom. ed.

Jer. 8:18 מבליגיתי עלי יגון — על דהוא מליעגין לקבל נבייא

דמתנבן להון דינא ותינחתא איתי עליהון מן קדם חוביהון עליהון אמר נביא לבי דוי.

It is a toseftoic addition which was probably intended for explanation. It can by itself in no way be read into the verse. It had replaced the original rendering, from which the last words remained. Com. T. to Am. 5:9

ib. 9:22 אל יתהלל חכם בחכמתו — שלמה בר דוד — לא ישתבח

חכימא בחוכמתיה ולא ישתבח — שמשון בר מנוח גברא בגבורתיה, ולא ישתבח אחאב בר עמרי עתירה בעותריה.

As regards the reference to Samson, the T. seemingly was influenced by Eccl. r. on 9:11. It appears on the margin of Cod. Reuch. under heading חא סא and is missing in the text.

ib. 10:11 כדנה תאמרון להום — רנא פשתנן אגרתא דשלח

ירמיה נביא לות שאר סבי גלותא די בבבל ואם יימרון לכון בסדאי (עממיא) ראתון ביניהון פלחו לטעותא בית ישראל כדון תתיבו וכדון תאמרון להון טעון דאתון פלחין להון טעות דלית בהון צרוך אינון מן שמיא לא יכלין לאחתא מטרא מן ארעא לא יכלין לצמחא פרין אינון ופלחיהון ייבדון מארעא וישתיצון מן תחות שמיא אלין.

This rhetorical exposition appears in all editions. In the Cod. Reuch. it appears after the literal Aramaic of the verse. In all other editions the Aramaic is omitted. Its position in the former testifies to its being an incursion, while is position in the latter

demonstrates, as another instance, how the original was forced
out by the interpolation.

ib. 12:5 ... כי את רגלים רצתה — ואם על טבון דאנא מוטב
לנבוכדנצר מלכא דבבל רגלאה נביא, את חזי ומתמיה ומן פון דאחזינך
מה דאנא עתיד למעבר לאהבתך צדיקיא דמן עלמא דרהטו בסוסותא
למעבד עובדין טבין קדמי ואף אמרית להון דאיתי על בניהון ברכן נחמן
הא כמיא דנחתין שטוף לירדנא.

This part appears in all editions after the complete rendering
of the v. Hence it is toseftoic. It is found fully in San. 96a:
כי את רגלים רצתה . . אף אתה ומה בשכר ארבע פסיעות ששלמתי
לאותו רשע שרץ אחרי כבודי אתה תמיה, כשאני מישלם שכר לאברהם
יצחק ויעקב שרצו לפני בסוסים על אחת במה ובמה.
Com. also San. 26a, Cant. r. כמעט שעברתי with minor changes.

ib. 31:14 קול ברמה נשמע — קול ברום עלמא — כדנן אמר יי'
אשתמע בית ישראל דבכן ומתאנחן בתר ירמיה כד שלח יתיה נבוזראדן
רב קטוליא מרמתא.

It contains a shortened Agada found in Lam. r. Pesichta, end.
That it does not belong here is evident from the two renderings of רמה one being literal, the other expository. Which of
them belongs to the original is difficult to determine; probably
the former.

Ezek. 1:1 ...ויהי — והוה בתלתין שנין לזמן דאישכח חלקיה כהנא
רבא ספרא דאוריתא בבית מקדשא בעזרתא תחות עולמא — בפלגות
...ביומי — לילא בתר מעלני סיהרא The portion after the horizontal
line is missing in the Targum of the Haftora of the first day
of the Feast of Weeks in the Machzor Witri. As the Targum
to this verse beginning לזמן and ending סיהרא is Midrashic in
construction and matter, its partial omission in Machzor Witri
lends support to the hypothesis that the whole portion is an
interpolation.

ib. 6 וארבעה פנים לאחת וארבע כנפים לאחת להם — וארבעא
אפין לחרא וארבעא אפין לכל חד וחד שתת עסר אפין לבריתא חדא מנין
אפיא דארבע ברין שתין וארבעא אפין — וארבעא אפין לחדא וארבעא
נפין לכל חד וחד שתת עסר נפין לכל אפא ואפא שתין וארבעא נפין
לבריתא חדא והוו מנין נפיא דארבע ברין מאתן וחמשין ושתא נפין.
The whole portion preceded by the horizontal line is missing
in the Ant. Polyg. having instead of the second וארבעא אפין —
וארבעא נפין. It also is a case of shortened toseftoic Targum.

‎...למזרק על אתר רשיעיא לאבד חיביא — וידי אדם... ib. 8
‎עברי מימריה — ולקבלא בהון תיובתא דכל בעלי תיובתא. This addition is found in the Ant. Polyg. only. Com. Pesachim 119a:
‎אמר ר"ש בן לקיש משום ר' יהודא נשיא מאי דכתיב וידי אדם...
‎ידו כתיב זה ידו של הקב"ה שפרוסה תחת כנפי החיות כדי לקבל
‎בעלי תשובה. In Machzor Witri (ib.) there is the following
addition prefacing the literal rendering of the Targum to v. 12:
‎וכד חזא יחזקאל נבייא ית חזוונא דאחזי ליה שכינתא הי כמא דאחוי
‎לישעיה בר אמוץ נבייא בהיכלא רחזא ארבע בריין דכוונין חד לקביל
‎חבריה לאחזאה עינוותנותיה וכן הוה תיקוניהון מהדרין אפא בקשוט —
‎ובריא... It is found nowhere else.

‎כל עתרא גיותא ויקרא — כל אבן יקרה מסכתך ib. 28:13
‎מתיהב לך. The literal translation was preserved in the toseftoic
version of this verse found on the margin of Cod. Reuch.,
entitled ‎ספ' אח, namely,‎ כל אבנן טבן.

‎בכן פרנסיא רשיעיא — תובו לאוריתא — לכן רעים ib. 34:9
‎ואנא עתיד לרחמא עליכון אציתון לאולפין — בכן פרנסיא קבלו פתגמא.
It is missing in Cod. Reuch.

A Midrashic Targum to 37:1 is found in Machzor Witri
in the Targum to the Haftora of the Sabbath of Passover:
‎והא דין גרמייא דנפקו ממצרי' בכוהון דלא איעכבו עד זמן קיצו דיי'
‎והוה גברא במצרי' ליומא ההוא ושמיה יאיר והוא הוה רב שיבטא
‎דבית אפרים אמר להון בעידנא ההוא כולהון בית ישר' הוו קיימין
‎בעינויא ובפולחנא קשיא ואנן הכי הוינא עברין יתהון מאתן ואלפין
‎גברין בני חילא ונפקו ממצרים ואתגאו בלא פורקנא דיי' ובכן מסרינון
‎יי' ביד מלכא דגת וקטל יתהון גנן ועבדוהי ואשרייני בגוי ההיא בקעתא
‎ובזמן פורקנא לא דבר יי' ית ישר' בההיא בקעתא דלמא יזעזעון.
This is told in San. 92a; Pirke d. E. 58. It is so interpreted
in Ps. Jon., Exod. 13:17.

‎ושלמתי לכם את השנים אשר אכל הארבה הילק Joel 2:25
‎ואשלם לכון שניא טבתא חלף שניא דבזו יתכון פלחי — והחסיל והגזם
‎כוכביא אומיא ולישניא ושלטוניא פורענות חילי רבא.
It is a latter Midrash. Com. Seder Eliahu r. 20 (p. 113):
‎כל גוים הנשארים בארץ לימות המשיח הולכין לארץ-ישראל ומביאים
‎כר לחם ומזון לתוך בתיהם של ישראל . . . ואומר אשר אכל הארבה...
‎אילו ארבע מלכיות שנשתעבדו בהן יישראל.
But 1:4 is rendered literally, and such was the case here, which

was displaced by the interpolation from which was left only the last part פורענות חילי רבא דשליחית בכון. This part has scarcely any connection with the interpolated exposition.

Nahum 1:1 משא נינוה — מטל כם דלוט לאשקאה ית נינוה —
מלקדמין אתנבי עלה יונה בר אמתי נביא דמנת חפר ותבת מחובהא ובדי
דאוסיפת למחטי תב ואיתנבי עלה נחום מבית קושי כמה דכתיב בספרא
הדין.

This is toseftoic. It has displaced the original Targum to the second half of the v. It is a late one. Witness the rendering מבית קושי by האלקישי being evidently influenced by the Arabic, the vernacular of the age. In the edition used by Rashi the reading was דמבית אלקיש. Com. the rendering of המרשתי Mi. 1:1.

Hab. 3:1 צלותא דצלי חבקוק נביא כד איתנלי ליה על ארכא
דיהב לרשיע הוא חבקוק נביא דצר צורתא וקם בנוה עני כן אמר חי
וקיים שמיה לית אנא עדי מן צורתא הדא עד דחוין לי על ארכא דיהבת
לרשיעיא מתיבא רוחא דקודשא וכן אמר ליה לחבקוק נביא על עיסק
ארכא דיהבת לרשיעיא דאם יתובון לאוריתא בלבב שלם ישתביק להון
ויהון כל חוביהון דחבו קדמוהי בית ישראל הא בישלותא.

Com. Shochar Tob 7, 17, ed. Buber.

וכשבא חבקוק אמר על משמרתי אעמודה ואתיצבה על מצור מהו מצור
מלמר שצר צורה ועמד בתוכה ואמר איני זז מכאן עד שתודיעני דבר זה...
This Agadic interpolation is found in the Cod. Reuch., of which Buber had no knowledge. It is missing in all other editions. Rashi (Taanith 23a), refers to it: כדמפרש בתרגום של תפלת חבקוק. The manner in which this reference is expressed would suggest that Rashi refers to the Targum of the Haftora of the second day of the Feast of Weeks, which was customary to read in the communities of Northern France. It is found in the Machzor Witri. On the other hand, it appears that Kimchi had no knowledge of this Targum. Probably the portion beginning על ארבא to the end, which is found in all editions, is a part of this T. J., the original being replaced by it.

ib. 2 שמעתי שמעך יראתי — י' שמעית שמע גבורתך —
מה רעבדתא בטופנא מן בראשית — ודחלתי ; — ואף על מחת פורענותא
דאייתיתא על אינשי סדום כד ארניזו קרמך שמעית וזעית י' — כמה
רברבין... — בגו רוגזך דאדגיזתא על רשיעיא וצדיקיא... — בנו רונזך...
ותרחם עליהון.

These exegetical interpolations are found in the Targum of the Haftora of the second day of the Feast of Weeks in the Machzor Witri. They are not found in any other accessible edition of the Targum. In verse 8 the words על מלכיא הוה רוגזך which is evidently the rendering of אם בנהרים אפך, and which are found in all editions, are missing there.

אף במעברך נסין ליהושע — שמש ירח עמד זבלה 3:11 .ib
במישר גבעון –- כד איתגברו וסליקו עלוהי חמשה מלכין מלכא דידושלם
מלכא דחבדון מלבא דירמות מלכא דלכיש מלכא דעגלון ; שמשא וסיהרא
קמו במדוריהון — תלתין ושית שען.
The portions following the horizonal lines are found in Cod. Reuch. and in Machzor Witri only. The same Targum was used, it would appear, by the editor of the text of the other editions, who shortened it. That the original rendering was a literal one is evident from the comparison of these two texts.

ואשפך על בית דוד ועל יתבי ירושלים רוח נביאה 12:10 .Zech
וצלותא דקישוט ומן בתר כרן יפוק משיח בר אפרים לאנחא קרבא עם
גוג ויקטול יתיה גוג קדם תרעא דירושלם ויסתכלון לותיה ויבעון מניה
מטול מא דקרו עממיא למשיח בר אפרים ויספדון עלוהי כמא דספדין
אבא ואמא על בר יחידאי ויתמרדו עלוהי כמה דמתמרדן על בוכרא.
This Midrashic Targum is found in Kenn., Cod. 154, and on the margin of Cod. Reuch., giving the source as תרג' ירוש and in Machzor Witri. It is omitted in all other editions. It will be seen that the Midrashic interpretation is based mainly on the portion וספרו עליו כמספר על היחיד which, according to this interpretation, refers to the violent death of the first Messiah, namely the son of Ephraim or Joseph. On the other hand, the rendering preceding and following it is close to the text but differs slightly from the rendering of the Targum. As to the Midrashic interpretation in general, com. Suk. 52a, Yer. 5, 8.

Two more cases of later interpolation may be added. The first is in Judges 10:16 ותקצר נפשו בעמל ישראל . It is rendered literally. In the Ant. Polyg. the Targum here has the Hebrew text. Maimonidas (Moreh Nebuchim 2, 29) makes it plain that this portion was not rendered by Jonathan for anthropomorphic considerations. The other case is Ezek. 1:26, which Kimchi (l. c.) says that it is not rendered by the T., but all

accessible editions do have a literal rendering. It was inserted by a later hand. The same may have also been the case
with Ezek. 1:27; 2:8, containing a peculiarly cirmumscribed
rendering.

II.

There is a considerable number of other interpolations
which are of an exegetical character. Some are recensions of the
rendering of the T. Others aim at a clarification not so much
of the text as of the rendering. They have a disturbing effect
upon the rendering. Evident interpolations of this category are
numerous. I have selected some of the most characteristic instances for the purpose of illustration. Finally I wish to call
attention that some of these duplicates were brought to notice
by Frankel (Zu Dem Targum d. Propheten, pp. 39, 40).

Duplications

אניח לעמי ישראל (ואשקיט להון) — אשקוטה   IS. 18:4

קרתא דבית שמש דעתידה למחרב — עיר החרס   ib. 19:18
One takes הרסת, הרם while the other would have it as it stands.
This passage of the T. is cited in Menahoth 110a; this duplicate
then is of a comparatively early date. It was noticed by Frankel
Zu Dem T., 40).

מריקו (וצחצחו) זינא — משחו מגן   ib. 21:5

אתיב לשכנתא מלותכון — ובל יאמר שכן חליתי   ib. 33:24
אתת עלנא מחת מדע.
According to one the refernce is to the absence of the Shekina;
the other is a simpler rendering.

הא לעבדי אוריתא סגי ישׄלמך קדמך ואת—הנה לשלום   ib. 38:17
מייתי מרירא לרשיעיא בכן בר ידעית יום מותי שפיכת דמעתי בצלו
קדמך מר לי סגי.
The latter is an interpolation. It disagrees with the interpretation of the T. of הנה לשלום referring to the pious ones. That
the entire phrase: מר לי מר is rendered by the latter is evident
from the rendering — מר לי סגי.

ובכרכרן — ובתושבחן — ובכרכרות   ib. 66:20
However ובכרכרן is missing in Cod. Reuch.

עומר ארמותא—כדמעה ארמות עללא—וכשירו חציר   Jerem. 2:3
In the former Israel is likened to the priestly tithe, in the latter
to the first ripened of the produce before the offering of the
Omer (Com. Rashi and Kimchi l. c.).

יקטלון גבורך — ויבזון נכסך — ירעוך קדקד   ib. 2:16.

— אתקבלא תושלמת עובדיכון — הגלת שלומים   ib. 13:19
גלו שלמא .
In the former שלומים is taken in the sense of שלם ; in the latter
שלם — pay.

ארי בזמן דאנא — בכי ומצוח — כי מדי אדבר אזעק   ib. 20:8
מתנבי אנא מרים קלא.

ועל דברן קים אבהתכון קדמי — ואעבר עליך ואראך   Ezek. 16:6
— אתגליתי למפרקכון, ארי גלי קדמי ארי אתון . . .

. ובכן פרנסיא — רשיעיא — לכם הרעים   ib. 34:9
The former read רעים ; the latter רעים . This was noticed by
Kimchi. The T. renders רעים throughout this chapter by פרנסיא
In Lag. רשיעיא is omitted.

. בית מקדשא — רבותא דיעקב — גאון יעקב   Am. 6:8
The last is the rendering in 8:7; the former is a duplicate.

יתפלשון בקטמא — חפו רישיהון — עפר התפלשתי   Mica 1:10
In Cod. Reuch. יתפלשון is omitted.

. גלן עריא — ערטילאין בהתין — עריה בשת   ib. 11
The latter is more literal.

עבידו לכון מספר בית צולאי — מספר בית האצל   ibid.
— בתי חמדתכון דהויתון אנסין ומקרבין דין לסטר דין, בכין...
The former renders האצל as a p. n., while the latter as אצל,
near. Com. Rashi and Karo l. c.

ומסברא — ומסברא למיתב לאוריתא — כי חלה לטוב   ib. 12 . לטב.

— יסקון משיזבין כד בקדמיתא — עלה הפרץ לפניהם   ib. 2:13
ויסק מלך מדבר בדישיהון.
The former renders פרץ—משיזבין deliverers and לפניהם—בראשונה,

the former, as in the former days, while the latter understood
פרין as king and לפניהם, in their front.

ib. 3:6   ...עמדי — אתגלי ואזיע ארעא בחוביהון בן בלבלינון
לעממיא — ואיתי מכולא על עם דרא ואף בתניתא כד חבו קדמוהי.
The recenssion, it is obvious, would render this v. in a symbolic
sense. The T. would render it literally. This is evident from
the literal rendering of what follows. On the other hand, the
inserted recenssion may constitute only a portion of a Toseftoic
rendering.

ib. 12 ...בזעם — באתגליותך — באתיותך לוט על סנאי עמך
למתבר רשעי ארעא.
Com. Rashi and Karo; as to the rendering of בזעם Com. Ze.
1:12; Mal. 1:4.

Zech. 3:7 ואתן לך רגליך מהלכין — ונתתי לך מהלכים —
ובאחיות מתיא אחיינך.
The inserted recenssion would render it symbolically.

ib. 3:8   הא אנא מיתי — ויתגלי — הנני מביא את עבדי צמח

Insertions

IS. 1:24 הוי אנחם מצרי — (ברם יי לרשיעיא בד אתגלי)

ib. 2:22 חדלו מן האדם אשר נשמה באפו — אתמנעו לכון
מלאשתעבדא לאנשא למעברה דחלא דנשמת רוח חיין באפוהו (ארי יומא
דין הוא קים ומחר ליתוהי) וכלמא חשיב הוא.

ib. 3:15 ופני עניים טחנו — (ומיתן — ואפי חשיכיא מבלון אתון
בריניהון).

ib. 5:3 ועתה יושב ירושלים ואיש יהורה שפטו נא ביני ובין
כרמי — (נביא אמר להון הא בית ישראל מרדו מן אוריתא ולא צבן
למיתב) כען יתבי . . .
The preceding passages of the T. make this rhetoric portion
entirely excessive.

ib. 24:1 ועוה פניה — (על דעברו על אוריתא) ותחפי בהתא
There is no more necessity for a reason here than there is for
the preceding בוקק את הארץ and the following והפיץ ישביה

ib. 30:25 פלגים יבלי מים — ביום קטול רב — (תקלא למלכין
ולמשריתיהון) פצירין נגדין מיין.

ib. 41:7 ויחזק הרש — דמתקיף — (הלא יבהתון בעובדיהון)
There is only one other such case, also evidently an interpolation,
this is Ez. 16:20. The T. as a rule knows of no such rhetorical
prefacing.

ib. 57:20 והרשעים כים נגרש — (יטרדו בגיהנם)
It is found in Cod. Reuch. only.

Jerem. 1:6 כי נער אנכי — ארי רבא אנא — (ובשירותי עקא
ועלו אנא מתנבי על עמא הדין).

ib. 2:10 כי עברו איי כתיים וראו — . . . והסתכלו לחדא וחזו
(עממיא רגלן מכרך לכרך וממדינה למדינה נטלין ית טעותהון ומובלין
להון עמהון ובאתר דאינון שרן פרסין ית משכניהון ומקימין ית טעותהון
וסגדין להון) אידא היא אומא . . .

ib. 2:27 ובעת רעתם — ובעירן דבשתא אתיא עליהון — (כפרין
בטעותיהון ו) מורן קדמי אמרין רחים עלנו.

ib. 4:1 אלי תשוב — (עד לא תתחתם גזירתך) תתקבל תיובתך
Com. 31; 17, 20.

ib 51:1 לב קמי — בסראי ארע יתבי ועל בבל על מיתי נא (הא
עממין קטולין) דרם לבהון ושפירין בקומא, רוחהון . . .

The insertion is in fact a duplicate interpretation of the former,
interpreting לב קמי to refer to the Chaldeans by the method of
Com. Karo, the latter takes it in a more literal sense.   אתבש

Ezek. 13:19 ...ולהמית נפשות — דימותון להון חזי דלא לאמתא
(לא אתון ממיתן) ולקימא נפשן דלא חזי להון לקימא.

Two different interpretations are here obviously incorporated.
In the London Polyg. the reading is: רימותון אתון ממיתן, דתתקומן
אתון מקומן.

Whether this was a correction by the editor due to misunderstanding or it represents a different reading, it adds emphasis
to the fact that the passages in question are insertions.

ib. 16:5 לרחמא — (חדא טבא לכון (למעבר לכון לאנהא
מישעבודכון לרחמא דילהון.

ib. 16:20 ותקחי — (ישראל בכנישת קדמי לארגזא איסגית (איכא
דרברית ית בנך...

ib. 17:4 שמו בכנענים בעיר — מפולחנא דבטלא לארעא ואיבליה
בארעא דבנען (ועד לא עלון בה בית ישראל) בקרית תגרין שויה.

Hos. 10:11 צוארה טוב על עברתי ואני — יתהון פרקית ואנא
משעבוד מצרים — אעריתי ניר תקיף מצוריהון.

Hos. 3:3 רבים ימים כי — רישראל בנשתא לה) אמר נביא
חוביכון גרמו לכון דתגלון) יומין סגיאין תתנהון לפולחני.

ib. 7:4 כלם... — לקימא דמוחן כמא מקרויהון בפריע יגלון (בכן
מחשבת רשע) ועל דלא אדברו נסין וגבורן דאתעבידו להון ביום מסקהון
ממצרים מערן מילש לישא עד לא חמא.

The inserted passage has no connection with the rest and renders
irritating the whole passage. Com. Rashi on this v.

ib. 12:1 אל עם רד עד ויהודה — מתקפין הוו יהודה ורבית
בפולחנא (עד רגלא עמא דאלהא מארעהון).

Joel 2:3 לו היתה לא פליטה וגם — ביה לית שיזבא ואף
(לרשיעיא).

דבדרי ביני פלחי מזריא... (סחור — אשר פזרו בגוים 4:2 .ib
סחור דארעא ישראל).

The inserted portion is found in extant editions, but is omitted
in all other editions, including the princeps edition of Mikraoth
Gedoloth.

מרי ניתי אנא ושקמין אית לי — כי בוקר אנכי 7:14 .Am
בשפלתא (מן קדם חובי דעמא ישראל אנא מסגיף נפשי).

בערנא ההיא אקום את מלכותא רבית דוד — ובניתיה... 9:11 .ib
דנפלת... ובניישתהון אתקין (ותשלט בכל מלכותא ותגמר ותשיצי סגי
משריתא) והיא תתבני ותשכלל...

This portion, intended for the last three words of the verse, is
to all intent a different version of a sort of a homily, examples of
which are readily presented in the portions of the interpolated
Targumim cited above. The original version seems to have been
replaced by the interpolation.

ארי הויתי כמיסף טביא — כי הייתי באספי קיץ 7:1 Mica
(בעדן דאבדו חסידיא מן ארעא).

The inserted passage is merely putting כמוסף טביא of the T.
in other words.

יום הוא ועדיך יבוא למני אשור ערי מצור ולמני 12 .ib
מצור ועד — בערנא ההיא יתכנישון גלותא דמן אתור קרוי תיקפא —
ודמן הורמני רבתא וקרוי צירא.

The latter part seems to me to belong to the first half of the v.
forming a different rendering, which was incorporated in the
T. to the second part of the v. and displaced the original. The
former renders מני as מן and אתור — אשור while the latter, impressed by the sound of the word, would render הורמני—למני,
Armenia. It was the same case with מצור   Aq. and Theod.
follow the first rendering of the T. The Lxx and P. are somewhat following the interpolated rendering.

בעלמא דהוא עתיד) -- עמא דאחסנתך — צאן נחלתך 7:14 .ib
לאיתחדתא) ישרון בלחודהון.

The inserted portion is entirely disconnected with the rest, has
no reference to any part of the v. It is explaining or com-

plementing the T. It was inserted with the intention of importing into this v. a Messianic air, while the T. might not have taken the v. in this sense.

(תדכר לנו עקידת — תתן אמת ליעקב חסד אברהם 7:20 ib.
יצחק דאתעקר על דבי מדבחא קדמך).

No reference is made in this v. to יצחק . The interpolator, it would appear, was anxious to supply this mossion.

(כד איתגלי כרחמתא למתן אוריתא — לפני זעמו Nahum 1:6
לעמיה כן זע עלמא מן קדמוהי) בכן...

It has no connection and makes no sense with what follows
It can be, however, connected with the preceding v. הרים רעשו
It is probably a recenssion of the rendering of the T. of that
v. and inserted at its end and then misplaced at the beginning
of this v.

ADDITIONS

Quotations from Targum Jonathan in Talmud and Midrash, like those from Onkelos, do not carry the name of the author to whom tradition ascribes the composition of the Targum. In most of the instances in Talmud Babli Targum Jonathan is quoted in the name of Rab Joseph. In two cases Rab Joseph himself quotes it, while in other cases the quotations are introduced by מתרגמינן. In one case in the Midrash the quotation from Jonathan carries the name of Aquila. In the rest of the cases there is no indication of the source. They are just the same quotations from Jonathan. Incidental similarity cannot serve as a basis for a contrary view, particularly when some of the quotations are of an exegetical nature.

Several quotations in Yerushalmi and Midrash, which I assumed to be a different version of the targumic rendering in the respective cases, were cited above. However, there are at least two cases in which the rendering of the Targum is clearly implied. One is Y. Shekalim 2, 6, with reference to Is. 33:21:

מכאן ואילך וימר אלף נחל אשר לא אוכל לעבור אפילו לבורנין גדולה אינה יכולה לעבור בו מ"ט וצי אדיר לא יעברנו.

This implies the rendering of the Targum of וצי. In Joma 77b the same exposition is accompanied by a quotation from the Targum.

The other case is Mech. יתרו, 9 with reference to Is. 21:9. which was quoted above (p. 29, note 43) from Gen. r., namely, ויש מחליפים בדבר נופלת זו מלכות בבל דכתיב בה נפלה בבל. It is based on the rendering of the Targum נפלת אף עתידא למיפל בבל. Had it not been based on the rendering of the Targum (which was well known to the scholar), there would certainly have followed a note giving the interpretation of the quotation from Is.

As regards the quotations from the Targum in Babli, it is well to notice that most of them represent interpretations of an expository nature. At least in two cases the quotations represent a different version of the targumic rendering.

146

Most of the quotations were referred to by De Rossi, Zunz and Frankel.

Quotations given in the name of Rab Joseph:

Moed Katan 26a on 2K 2:12 :

אביו ואמו ורבו שלימדו תורה מנלן דכתיב ואלישע רואה והוא מצעק
אבי אבי רכב ישראל ופרשיו, אבי אבי זה אביו ואמו, רכב ישראל
ופרשיו זה רבו שלימדו תורה מאי משמע כדמתרגם רב יוסף דטב להון
לישראל בצלותיה מרתיכין ופרשין.

Pesachim 68a on Is. 5:17 :

וחרבות מחים גרים יאכלו, מאי משמע, כדמתרגם רב יוסף ונכסיהון
דרשיעיא צריקיא יחסנון.

Menachoth 110a on Is. 19:18 :

מאי עיר החרס יאמר לאחת, כדמתרגם רב יוסף קרתא דבית שמש
דעתיד למחרב אתאמר דהיא חדא מנהון.

Joma 77b on Is. 33:21

יבול יעברנו בבורני גדולה ת"ל יצי אדיר לא יעברנו, מאי משמע,
כמדתרגם רב יוסף לא תזל ביה בספינת ציידין ובורני רבתא לא תגוזינה.

Aboda Zara 44a on Is. 41:16 :

ומאי משמע דהאי וישאם דוד, לישנא דזרויי הוא, כדמתרגם יוסף
תזרם ורוח תשאם ומתרגמינן תזרינון ורוח תטלטלינון.

The interpretation of 2S 5:21 is against the rendering there of the Targum. It seems that the Agadist would render וישאם דוד in the same sense as ורוח תשאם is rendered in the Targum, namely, and David scattered them. Other Agadists would adhere to the extant rendering of the Targum. Hence the quotation in Rosh Hashana 22b. In the instance here, however, the quotation is introduced by כדמתרגם רב יוסף and also by כדמתרגמינן, one of them is seemingly an interpolation.

Joma 32b on Jer. 46:20 :

מאי קרצו אמר עולא לישנא דקטלא הוא, אמר רב נחמן בר יצחק מאי
קרא עגלה יפה פיה מצרים קרין מצפון בא בא, מאי משמע, כדמתרגם
רב יוסף מלכותא יאי הוה מצרים עממין קטולין מצפונא ייתון עלה
למבזה.

Kiddushin 13a on Hos. 4:2 :

אלה וכחש ורצח וגנב ונאף פרצו בדמים נגעו, מאי משמע, כדמתרגם
רב יוסף מולידין בנין מנשי חבריהון חובין על חובין מוסיפין

Nedarim 38a on Am. 7:14 :

עמוס דכתיב ויען עמוס ויאמר אל אמציה לא נביא אנכי ולא בן נביא
אנכי כי בוקר אנכי ובולס שקמים, כדמתרגם רב יוסף ארי מרי גיתי
אנא וישקמין לי בשפלתא.

Baba Kama 3b on Ob. 1:6 :

איך נחפשו עשו נבעו מצפוניו, מאי משמע, כדמתרגם רב יוסף איכדין
איתבליש עשו איתגליין מטמרוהי.

Berakoth 28a on Zef. 3:18 :

אמר דיב"ל כל המתפלל תפלה של מוספין לאחר ארבע שעות לר' יהודה
עליו הכתוב אומר נוגי ממועד אספתי ממך היו, מאי משמע דהאי נוגי
לישנא דתברא הוא, כדמתרגם רב יוסף תברא אתי על סנאיהון דבית
ישראל על דאחרו זמני מועדי דבירושלם.

The saying of R. Jehoshua b. Levi is based on the rendering of the Targum of this verse, which is: דהוו מעכבין בך
זמני מועדך . The quotation here in the name of Rab Joseph
agrees in sense with the Targum but not in the wording. This
might be explained as being a misquotation. However, the
rhetorical prefacing phrase תברא אתי..., which is missing in
our text, seems to have been in the text of the Agadist. It
was this beginning of the rendering which, it would appear,
caused the complication with regard to the reference. For what
was wanted here was to show that נוגי means delay, and the
reference here is to the rendering of this particular word in
the Targum, namely, דהוו מעכבין . But because the Targum
of this verse had as the beginning the words תברא אתי the reference was made to תברא although it was dropped from the
Targum.

Kiddushin 72b on Zech. 9:6 :

אלא לר' יוסי מאי וישב ממזר באשדוד, כדמתרגם רב יוסף יתבון בית
ישראל לרוחצן בארעהון דהוו דמי בה לנוכראין.

This is also a different version of the Targum to this verse
Our Targum renders it: וייתבון בית ישראל באשדוד דהוו בה
כנוכראין.

Two quotations are said by Rab Joseph:

Sanhedrin 94b on Is. 8:6 :

א"ר יוסף אלמלי תרגומא דהאי קרא לא הוה ידענא מאי קאמר חלף
דקין עמא הדין במלכות דבית דוד דמדבר להון בניח במי שילוחא דנגדין
בנייח ואיתרעיאו ברצין ובן רמליהו.

Moed Katan 28b on Zech. 12:11 :

נענה ר' עקיבא ואמר, ביום ההוא יגדל המספד בירושלם כמספד הדרימון,
וא"ר יוסף אלמלא תרגומיה דהאי קרא לא הוה ידענא מאי קאמר בעדנא
ההיא יסגי מספרא בירושלם כמספרא דאחאב בר עמרי דקטל יתיה
הדרימון בר טברימון וכמספד דיאשיה בר אמון דקטל יתיה פרעה חגירא
בבקעת מגידון.

Quotations preceded by ומתרגימן :

Nazir, last Mishna, according to the version in Ein-Jakob,
on 1S 1:11

ומודה אל יעלה על ראשו, ומתרגמינן ומרות אנוש לא תהא עלוהי.

Rosh Hashana 22b on 2S 5:21

מאי משמע דמישעיאין לישנא דיקוד הוא דכתיב וישאם דוד ואנשיו,
ומתרגמינן ואוקדינון דור.

Moed Katan 2a on Is. 62:5

ומאי משמע דהאי בית הבעל לישנא דמייתבותא הוא דכתיב כי יבעל
בחור בתולה, ומתרגמינן ארי כמא דמייתתב עולם עם בתולתא יתוותבון
בגויך בנייך.

Quotations without reference to the Targum:

Sanhedrin 95a on Is. 10:32 :

א"ר הומא אותו היום נשתייר מעונה של נוב. אמרי ליה בלדאי אי אזלת
האידנא יכלת לה ואי לא לא יכלת לה. אודהא דבעא לסנויי בעשרה
יומי סגא בחד יומא. כי מטו לירושלם שדי ליה ביסתרקי, עד דסליק
ויתיב מעלוי שורה, עד דחזויה לכולה ירושלם. כי חזייה איזוטר בעיניה.
אמר הלא דא היא קרתא דירושלם דעלה ארגישית כל משריתי ועלה
כביישת כל מדינתא, הלא היא זעירא וחלישא מכל כרכי עממיא דכבשית
בתקוף ידי עלה. וקם ומניד ברישיה מוביל ומייתי בידיה על טור בית
מקדשא דבציון על עזרתא דבירושלם אמרי...

The portion beginning הלא דא is found in all editions of the
Targum, and has been considered above (p. 132). At any
rate, the portion beginning וקם ומניד is the targumic rendering
of the verse.

Shabbath 128a on Josh. 7:21 :

וארא בשלל ארדת שנער, ר' אסי אמר אסטלא דמילא.

The rendering of ארדת in Targum is איצטלא

A quotation of the Targum to Nahum 3, 8, preceded by
מתרגמינן in Gen. r. 1 :

אמון רבתא כמה דתימא החיטבי מנא אמון, ומתרגמינן האת טבא
מאלכסנדריא רבתא דיתבא בין נהרתא.

Ecc. r. 11, 3 quotes the Targum to Is. 5:6 in the name of Aquila:

תרגם עקילם הגר ועל העבים אצוה מהמטיר עליו מטר, ועל נביאיא
אפקר דלא יתנבאון להון נבואתא.

Y. Shabbath 6, 4 contains a translation of Is. 5:18-23. Some of the rendering coincide with those in the Targum, namely: השרות — הפארות—כלילא ; שידאין (Targum שירי ידיא). הטבעות—עיזקייא (Targum עזקתא). The rendering of הסהרונים — עונקיה follows the T. Jud. 8:21, to which reference is made (The T. here having סבכיא agrees with ל"א on the margin of Cod. Reuch. to Jud. l. c. having for עינקיא—סיבכיא). קרשיא as the rendering of והלחשים is the translation in the T. of בתי הנפש . There are good reasons for the supposition that this is a version of the Targum to these verses. Com. פני משה l. c.

Y. Taanith 2, 5:   א"ר לוי מהו ארך אפים רחיק רגיז.

The renrering of ארך אפים in the Targum to Joel 2:13 is מרחיק רגז . (Also On. Exod. 34:6; Ps. Jon. having ארך רוח). Psichta Lam. r. 16 on Jer. 4:18: ומי עשה לך דרכך ומעלליך: אורחתיך בישאתא ועובדיך מרידאתא . This agrees with the Targum except that the latter has instead of מרידאתא — מקלקליא . It is to be noticed that both this and the preceding citation contain exegetical renderings.

Lev. r. 6, 4: המצפצפים והמהגין אלין המציינין אלו רמנהמין Targum רמנצפין ודמנהמין .

Lev. r. 5, 2; Exod. r. 10:5 on Am. 6:4 מטות שן על ערסין . דשכבן על ערסן דמכבשן בשן רפיל Targum דפיל.

Can. r on Ez. 16:61 יחורה לבנות מהו ...יוחנן דר' רעתיה הוא לכופרנין.

This is the usual rendering of לבנות in the Targum (com. vv. 46, 48, 49, 57), although in this verse the rendering is לאשתמעא . R. Jochanan would have here also the usual rendering.

Finally, there is the use of טעוותא for idols in Yerushalmi and Midrashim. Com. Y. Berakoth 9, 1 אינון הבא וטעוותהון בבבל ; Y. San ואינון הבא וטעוותהון ברומי ואינון הבא וטעוותהון עמהון 10, 2: אוי לכם ולטעותכם . As טעוותא is the peculiar rendering in the Targumim of idols, it is reasonable to assume that

this descriptive term came into use in the Yerushalmi from
the Targum.

2.

The toseftoic portions which were examined in the chapter on Interpolated Targumim do not represent all the Midrashic additions to Targum Jonathan. Many more are to be
found in the commentaries of Kimchi, Rashi and other Rabbinical sources. A great number of fragmentary Targumim are
found on the margin of Cod. Reuch. All of which were col-
lected and elaborated by Bacher (Z. D. M. G., v. 28, p. 1
et seq.).

On close examination it will be found that those fragments on the margin of Cod. Reuch. which are headed by
ספ' אח', תרג' אח', תרג' ירוש' and תרג' ירוש' have many characteristic points
in common. Hence there is no ground for an insistence on
a line of division between them as is held by Bacher. They
may have a common source. Or, certain fragments in each
group may be assigned to an earlier date and a different source
than the rest. It will be noticed that the additions to the
Targum of Is. 49:24, 25, which in Cod. Reuch. is referred to
תרג' ירוש' is designated in the extant editions ת"א.

In the main, the fragments described as תרג' אח', תרג' ירוש'
and ספ' אח' contain current Agadic expositions. But while
to the group of תרג' ירוש' belong the larger portions,
there is hardly any peculiar characteristic either with regard
to material or language to justify its placing in a separate
category. Furthermore, all of them exhibit a dependence on
Targum Jonathan. So ירוש' on Judges 12:6 following Jon.
ואחרון ליה ונכסין ליה במניזת ירדנא ואיתקטלו... Com. also 5:4, 5
and on Josh. 14:15. It is quoting Jon. to 1K 8:27 and 2K 21:16
(Yerush. on Is. 66:6). As to ת"א and ס"א com. ת"א וס"א
on Jerem. 9:22 ...לא ישתבח שלמה בר דוד חכימא בחוכמתיה. ת"א
on Zech. 11:8 ושיציתי ית תלתא פרנסיא... ידחיק מימרי יתהון על
דנפשתהון קצא בפולחני. Also on Is. 45:7, which are so rendered
in Targum Jonathan.

All these groups contain fragments which either explain
or are complementing the rendering of Jonathan.

Yerush. וְהוא גברא חד לא מית בחוביה Josh. 22:20 on ירוש׳
Com. also on Judges 1:3. וְהוא יתרגם באבניא ומן בתרכן גברא חד

ת"א on Josh 6:1 דפרזלא ומתקפא כמה דמתרדיף on 1S 26:20 ס"א. בעברין דנחישא adds ת"א. ומתאחדא

כמה דדריף בר ניצוצא קוראה בטוריא complementing קוראה
Also explaining the Targum Josh 4:19 קדמאה לירחא — לירחא
דניסן.

So that there is scarcely any foundation for a supposition
that they represent three distinct sources. There is equally no
basis for a theory of an earlier Targum to the Prophets of
which the ספ׳ אח׳ or even ירוש׳ and ת"א are remnants.

Certain portions are admittedly late. Such, for instance as
Is. 49:24, 25 and its parallel on Is. 66:5 which have made their
way into the text of the Targum (the latter is found in the
first Bomberger edition). They bear the traces of the Arabic
era. The fact also that the ירוש׳ on 1S 17:8 interpreting
ואת ערבתם — וית נט פטורי is not quoted by Rab Joseph, the
author of this interpretation in Babli (Keth. 9b) shows that
this Targum was not known yet at that time. Then, their
dependence on Jon. and also on Onkelos (com. ירוש׳
on Judges 18,3 following Onk. Exod. 3:5; 32:1; Deut. 5:28;
23:4; Also ירוש׳ on 1S 17:8 ואם אתון אמרין על מימרא דד׳ מרי
נצחן קרבא, ה׳ איש מלחמה ...which is the rendering in Onk. of
Exod. 15:3) would tend to place their origination at a date
subsequent to that of the official Targumim.

However, although of a comparatively later date, they
have preserved some earlier and later displaced renderings of
the Targum. Here are the instances in the Yerushalmi:
במסאסא Jud. 3:31 חריפין .Jon ; טיזרין on Josh. 5:3 ירוש׳
5:4; ית דשר .Jon ; ית סיכת 4:21 : בפרש רתורי .Jon ; דתורי
; יצלח .Jon ; יחי מלכא 2K 11:12 ; מכו .Jon ; שמיא איתרביינו
.Jon ; חמון 13:21 : חזי .Jon ; פולמסיא משרית .Jon ; וטלקון
; פגרין .Jon ; שלדין 19:35 ; כתועבת .Jon ; כריחוק 16:3 ; ורמו
.Jon ; אדליקו בוצינא Is. 21:5 ; אישתיזבו : אפכו ib. 37
אקימו סכוואן. As for those in תר׳ אח׳, ספ׳ אח׳ com. Bacher l. c.

Lightning Source UK Ltd.
Milton Keynes UK
UKHW010405180223
417189UK00004B/208